Black
AND
British

A short, essential history

DAVID OLUSOGA

Macmillan Children

D0176902

First published 2020 by Macmillan Children's Books
an imprint of Pan Macmillan
The Smithson, 6 Briset Street, London EC1M 5NR
EU representative: Macmillan Publishers Ireland Ltd, 1st Floor,
The Liffey Trust Centre, 117–126 Sheriff Street Upper
Dublin 1, D01 YC43
Associated companies throughout the world
www.panmacmillan.com

ISBN 978-1-5290-6339-4

9

A CIP catalogue record for this book is available from the British Library.

Design: Perfect Bound Ltd
Editorial: Jo Foster

Printed and bound by CPI Group (UK) Ltd, Croydon CR04YY

CONTENTS

INTRODUCTION

When I was at school there was no Black history. None of the Black people from the past who we know about today were ever mentioned by my teachers, and my textbooks contained nothing about the role Black people have played in the story of Britain. So what I presumed was that there must not have been any Black people in British history.

It was only when I became a teenager, and was able to read grown-up history books, that I learned that there had been Black people throughout much of British history, all the way back to the Roman conquest. It was from then onwards that I learned about slavery and about the British Empire, about Black Tudors, like the trumpeter John Blanke, and Black people like Dido Elizabeth Belle and Oludah Equiano who lived in Britain in the eighteenth century. I also learned about the Black children who lived as slaves in the houses of rich people in London, Bristol, Liverpool and other cities. I read about the enslaved people who were made to work on plantations in the West Indies and America, and learned how the sugar and cotton they grew helped make Britain rich. I discovered that there had been Black sailors at the Battle of Trafalgar and that Black soldiers had fought in the trenches of the First World War. I read about the Black pilots and navigators who served in the Royal Air Force during the Second World War and about the people who had come to Britain on the *Windrush* in 1948 to start new lives.

A few years ago I wrote a book for grown-ups about Black British history. Ever since I finished that book, young people and their parents have been asking me to write a book like this one. A book for younger readers. This is the book I wish I had been given to read when I was at school. I have written it so that the history of Black people in Britain can be read by everybody, and not just grown-ups. This book is an introduction. It is a place to start learning about Black British history and it will introduce you to some of the thousands of Black people who made their homes in Britain in past centuries.

One thing I was taught about in my schools was the Industrial Revolution. What I was taught is probably what you have been taught. I learned about the huge factories that were built in the North of England, and parts of Scotland, Wales and Ireland. I learned about the rich men who owned them and I was taught about the new machines they invented, like the Water Frame, the Flying Shuttle and the Spinning Jenny. I was also taught about the children who had to work in the factories that made the new products of the Industrial Age and the mills that produced the clothes everyone wore.

Two of the most important products of the Industrial Revolution were cotton cloth and cotton yarn (thread) made in the mills using the new machines. At my school I learned about how the cotton that had been picked from cotton plants was transformed into cloth and yarn. But what I was not told by my teachers, and what was not mentioned in my school textbooks or in any of the museums we visited on school trips, was where the cotton come from before it arrived in the mills.

Most of that cotton came from the Mississippi Valley, in the Deep South of the United States of America. It was grown on plantations by Africans, men and women who were enslaved. By the middle of the nineteenth century, when Queen Victoria was on the throne, 1.8 million African-Americans worked growing cotton in the United States. Much of that cotton was sent on ships across the Atlantic Ocean to Britain. The ships sailed up the River Mersey and into the docks of Liverpool. From there it was sent to the thousands of mills in Lancashire in the north of England – the part of the country around

Manchester. The Black people who were enslaved in America made the Mississippi Valley one of the richest places in the world. But they also made Manchester and Lancashire Valley wealthy. The cotton mills in and around Manchester made the city so rich that it was given a nickname – Cottonopolis.

Today we remember the Industrial Revolution for the hard, difficult work of our ancestors who worked in the factories and mills. But we have forgotten the almost 1.8 million Black men and women of the American South who lived and died as slaves to grow the cotton. The enslaved people of the Deep South never set foot in Britain but they are part of British history. This is just one example of the ways in which the histories of Black people have often been missed out of the British history we learn at school.

Since I wrote the grown-up version of this book, new discoveries have been made and new Black Britons from earlier generations have been found in old documents stored in archives. Black British history is growing. We know more with each passing year. In recent years we have learned about Jacques Francis, the enslaved Black diver who led a diving expedition that attempted to salvage items from the *Mary Rose*, Henry VIII's flagship, after it had sunk. We have also learned more about the lives of enslaved people living in Georgian Britain, thanks to a project at Glasgow University that has searched the archives to find more than 800 advertisements that were placed in British newspapers by slave owners offering rewards for the return of enslaved people who had run away. Through those advertisements we learned more about the ages, appearances, clothing and skills of enslaved Black people living in Britain more than 200 years ago.

With each passing year, Black British history is not only expanding, it is also becoming ever more personal to increasing numbers of people. Britain's population is changing. More of us than ever are members of families that include people of different skin colours and ethnicities. Black history helps explain how national history is intertwined with our family histories. It helps us make sense of the country we are today.

ROMANS

27 BC–476 AD

Africans first came to Britain with the Roman Empire. Long before Britain began to build its own empire, it was invaded and conquered by the Romans in the year 43 AD. Britain became a region on the edge of the mighty empire of Rome, which stretched across Europe, North Africa and the Middle East.

When we talk about Romans, we don't just mean people from Rome or Italy. Roman citizens could come from anywhere in the empire. People from all over the empire and even beyond travelled

> Roman citizens could come from anywhere in the empire

huge distances to trade, work, and fight in the Roman army. We know that Africans lived and settled in Roman Britain. By the time the Romans had been here for 200 years, some places in Britain may even have had a more diverse population than they do today.

Who were the Aurelian Moors?

The first recorded group of Africans living in Britain were soldiers in the Roman army. They came to defend the edge of the empire at Hadrian's Wall.

The wall stretched for more than seventy miles, right across what is now northern England. It was built in the years after 120 AD by order of the Emperor Hadrian. He wanted a border for the empire in Britain, to control who could come in from the north and to defend against tribes who might attack. Soldiers were stationed in forts and watchtowers along the wall. Those soldiers came from all over the empire – and so did their families, their commanders, and traders who sold them whatever they needed.

In 1934, Latin words were found carved into a stone in a village in Cumbria, north-west England. They said that a group of soldiers called the 'Aurelian Moors' had been stationed at the nearby fortress of Aballava between the years 253 and 258 AD. The word 'moors' means 'people

There are still long stretches of Hadrian's Wall that you can walk along today.

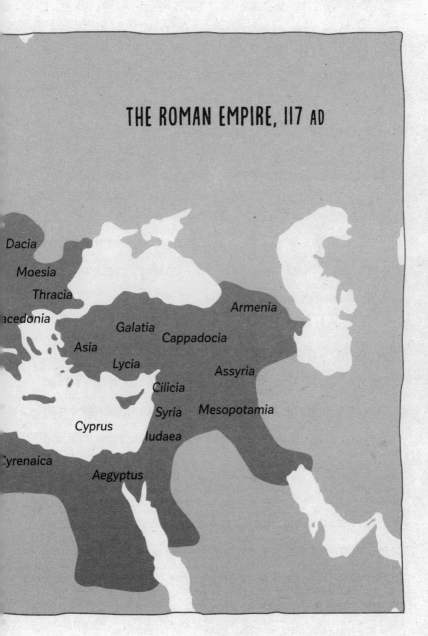

THE ROMAN EMPIRE, 117 AD

Dacia

Moesia

Thracia

acedonia

Galatia

Asia

Lycia

Armenia

Cappadocia

Cilicia

Assyria

Syria

Mesopotamia

Cyprus

Iudaea

yrenaica

Aegyptus

from North Africa', the part of the empire where the soldiers came from. They were named 'Aurelian' after the Emperor Marcus Aurelius. There is another mention of the Aurelian Moors of Aballava in a list of Roman officials' travel, which confirms that they were there.

Aballava wasn't just a fort – it was a whole community. As well as soldiers and officers, other people from across the empire would have lived in Aballava, including the soldiers' families.

How do historians know what Romans looked like?

Romans didn't think and write about race and skin colour in the same way we do today. But historians and archaeologists can piece together clues to show that the Romans in Britain were black and brown, as well as white.

We can read what Romans wrote about where people came from in histories, records of the army, and carvings on tombs. We can also study the skeletons they left behind. Archaeologists today can use forensic science to find new clues in skeletons, some of which were dug up more than a hundred years ago.

Isotope analysis means studying the chemicals left in bones and teeth by what a person ate and drank as a child. By matching levels of these chemicals in different places, archaeologists can find clues to where the person grew up.

Craniometrics means measuring bones and skulls to find patterns which can be matched with skeletons from different parts of the world. It can help to work out if someone was probably from a European, African or mixed-race family.

Using chemical analysis and bone measurements, archaeologists are learning that Roman Britain was much more diverse than we used **Roman Britain was much more diverse than we used to think** to think. We can't know exactly how many people with dark or light skin lived in Roman Britain, but we can be certain that people from Africa lived here more than 1,700 years ago.

Archaeologists studying skeletons from Roman Britain have found many which appear to be African. The length of some Roman skeletons' limb bones gave twentieth-century archaeologists a clue that they may have been Black Africans. When archaeologists in the twenty-first century studied over 200 Roman skulls found in York, they found that hunch was right: in fact, more than one in ten of them had features similar to people with African ancestors.

Ivory Bangle Lady

'Ivory Bangle Lady' is the name historians gave to one Roman African whose skeleton was found in York. She was a young woman who died in the third century. Ivory Bangle Lady was discovered buried in a stone coffin, called a sarcophagus. She had expensive luxuries buried with her: jewellery made from silver, bronze, bone and coloured glass, a mirror, and a perfume bottle. She also

The jet and ivory bracelets found in York.

had black and white bracelets. The black bangles were made of jet, which probably came from north-east England, and the white bangles were made of ivory, probably from Africa. Perhaps the ivory was a reminder of home.

When archaeologists measured Ivory Bangle Lady's skull, they found it was similar to skulls of people with Black and white ancestors. And when they studied the chemical isotopes in her bones, they found she hadn't grown up in York. Instead, she could have spent her childhood somewhere like North Africa. Putting all the clues together, Ivory Bangle Lady was most likely a mixed-race woman with a North African background. She was also from a high social class.

It wouldn't have seemed odd to a Roman that Ivory Bangle Lady was both African and rich. The skeletons of Black Romans have been found in York in places where both rich and poor people were buried. For Romans, skin colour didn't determine your place in society.

For Romans, skin colour didn't determine your place in society

The Roman Empire in Western Europe crumbled in the fifth century. When the Romans left Britain, the paths between Britain and Africa were wiped away. In the next thousand years, only tiny numbers of Africans came to Britain. For most British people, Africa lived on in stories from the Bible and from Greek and Roman writers, with myths mixed in with truth. From the Greeks and Romans who had travelled to Africa, medieval Europeans knew that people from Africa had dark skin, and they knew the rough shape of the continent. But they could also read fantastic stories about places in Africa where there were diamonds lying on the ground for anyone to pick up; a fountain with water that kept people young forever; and strange people who had the heads of dogs, or had just one eye in the middle of their foreheads. This picture, of a headless man called a 'Blemmye,' is shown in Africa on the famous medieval map of the world, the *Mappa Mundi*.

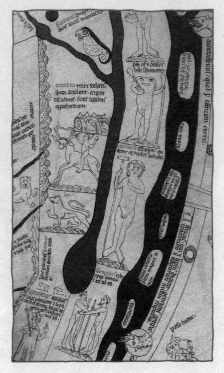

Until new sea routes started to give Europeans a way to get to Africa directly, most of the continent would stay a mystery to them.

The location of the Blemmye on the Mappa Mundi. The map shows the world as it was understood in around 1300; Jerusalem at the centre, and Africa on the right.

TUDORS

1485-1603

You hardly ever see Black people in films and pictures of Tudor England – but they were there. Historians have dug through the archives to find the names and stories of hundreds of Black Tudors.

John Blanke – trumpeter at the court of Henry VIII

If you've learned about Henry VIII and his six wives at school, you'll know how desperate he was to have a son. When his first wife, Catherine of Aragon, had a baby boy in 1511, Henry was delighted. He didn't know that the baby prince would only live for a few weeks. The King threw a huge party to celebrate the birth. The Westminster

The royal trumpeter John Blanke depicted on the Westminster Tournament Roll, 1511.

Tournament went on for two days, with processions and jousting, and Henry ordered artists to paint a picture of the whole event on a scroll known as the Westminster Tournament Roll. There are two parts which show trumpeters, playing at the opening and closing of the tournament. Both of them very clearly show the face of a black man among the uniformed musicians. We know from court accounts that there was a 'blacke trumpeter' in the court of Henry VIII and his father Henry VII, and that his name was John Blanke. He is the earliest Black person in Britain whose name and face we know.

We know other parts of John Blanke's story, too. John played for the Tudor royal family for years, and was right at the centre of historic royal events. He played at King Henry VII's funeral, and at his son Henry VIII's coronation. John even wrote to Henry VIII to ask for a pay rise, so that he would be on the same level as the other trumpeters. When John got married, the King sent him a new outfit as a wedding present.

The Royal Household

John Blanke was one of several hundred Black Tudors historians have found in the records. Many of them probably came to Britain from Spain and Portugal, countries with more contact and trade with Africa than England had. Henry VIII's first wife, Catherine of Aragon, was Spanish. When she first came to England in 1501, she brought a whole group of servants and followers with her, including Africans. Catherine wasn't the only European royal to have Africans working for her. There was a fashion at the time for Africans in royal courts, especially as musicians. Having Africans as part of their households let rich Europeans show off their international connections, and let everyone know that they were part of the sophisticated modern world.

> There was a fashion at the time for Africans in royal courts

Over the years when the Tudor kings and queens were on the throne, British merchants began to trade with Africa and even to take enslaved Africans across the Atlantic. As those journeys increased, more and more Africans arrived in Britain. Most Black Tudors in Britain were not slaves. They had ordinary lives and jobs, often working as servants. They married local people, and had children. Later on, once Britain had built up its slave trade and its slave-owning colonies in America and the Caribbean, people began to assume that slaves were Black people but that idea did not exist in Tudor England and Stuart Scotland.

The Age of Discovery

The Tudor period was part of Europe's 'Age of Discovery', when sailors began to explore the world and to brave far-off and mysterious oceans. That included the seas around most of Africa. British ships were not the first to begin sailing directly from Europe to West Africa. A century before English sailors started making the journey, Portugal sent ships to explore the unknown African seas south of the Mediterranean.

Portuguese sailors had the most advanced ships, and they used science learned from the Muslim world to find their way. Bit by bit, by order of the King of Portugal, they inched their way around the coast of Africa. They ventured further and further south, occasionally bringing back interesting finds.

The Portuguese explorers set out to find the wonders of Africa they had read about in ancient travellers' tales, and they also wanted to get rich. The African kingdoms had many valuable goods to trade, like dyewood, ivory and pepper. Most of all, the explorers wanted African gold. Once they could buy gold from West Africans on the coast and take it straight to Europe in ships, they no longer had to rely on the Muslim traders who crossed the Sahara desert. They built up their trade with Africa and shut out other European countries. By the 1460s the Portuguese had built a base on an island off the coast of Mauritania, which they used to trade with the local Africans.

When the English heard about the wealth the Portuguese were bringing back from Africa, it sounded too good to miss out on. In the 1530s, English traders started to make journeys to the parts of West Africa where the Portuguese had built up their trade.

How did English trade with Africa begin?

The first man to try was William Hawkins from Devon, a merchant who was used to trading with France and Spain. Hawkins set sail for Africa in the 1530s, and then took goods from Africa to sell in Brazil.

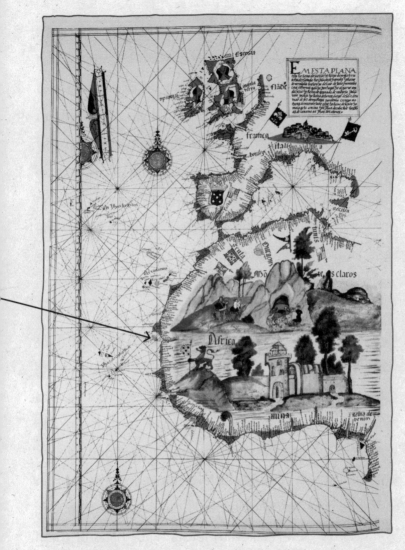

Map of Western Africa by Luis Lázaro (1563). The large castle in West Africa is Elmina Castle in present-day Ghana – the first European building in sub-Saharan Africa.

The next English sea captain to try to break in to Portugal's trade with Africa was Thomas Wyndham. Wyndham was a former pirate, who didn't mind a bit of robbery and violence to go with his business deals. He had an important advantage: his second-in-command, Anthony Anes Pinteado, was Portuguese. Pinteado was an experienced captain, who came to England after making powerful enemies in Portugal. He knew how to sail the seas around West Africa, and how much money there was to be made there.

Pinteado and Wyndham set out for Africa in 1553. Their voyage was paid for by London merchants and by King Edward VI. Thomas Wyndham went to trade, but he also attacked Portuguese ships and stole from them. He managed to trade with the Africans for gold and pepper, but then made his big mistake: he didn't listen when Pinteado said they should head home. As they sailed on, Wyndham's crew fell ill with fevers. Two-thirds of them died before they made it back to London – including both Wyndham and Pinteado. Still, the voyage was a business success. The merchants who had paid for it were happy with the profit they made, and they could see that trading with Africa would be worth the risk.

The five men of Shama

A few months later, the merchants paid for another voyage. This time, the captain's name was John Lok, and his mission was more successful than Wyndham's. He took three ships to the Gold Coast (now Ghana), managed to make it home alive, and brought back pepper, ivory and – most importantly – lots of gold. He also brought back five African men from the village of Shama. We know the English names that three of them used: Anthonie, Binnie and George. The men from Shama spent a few months in London before going home. The plan was that now they had learned English and gone back to Africa, they would be interpreters and help English traders make deals with the locals.

If the English wanted African gold, they needed to learn to work with experienced African traders. The West African kingdoms were strong, rich, and had been trading with outsiders for centuries. They knew exactly how valuable their gold was. The kingdoms the Tudor explorers hoped

West African kingdoms were strong, rich, and had been trading with outsiders for centuries

to deal with included the Oyo empire in modern Nigeria; Dahomey, in modern Benin; the Akan people, who lived near the coast of modern Ghana; and the empire of Benin in modern Nigeria. The Oba (kings) of Benin were especially rich and powerful, and ruled from a magnificent

palace in Benin City. You can see many beautiful brass decorations from the Oba palace in museums in Europe and America, because more than 300 years later, Victorians from Britain came to Benin and took them. But in John Lok's time, English merchants were no match for the armies of the West African kingdoms.

The Voyages of John Hawkins

The Tudors never did manage to take control of the African gold trade from the Portuguese. Instead, some English traders found another way to make a profit. They

A bronze plaque that once decorated the palace of the Oba of Benin, modern-day Nigeria.

knew that the Spanish and Portuguese were buying slaves in Africa, and taking them across the Atlantic to work in Spanish and Portuguese colonies in the Americas. John

Spanish and Portuguese galleons proved easy targets for British buccaneers.

Hawkins, an English merchant, tried to copy this idea. He made three trips to West Africa, where, as well as trading, he attacked Portuguese ships and captured the enslaved Africans he found on board. Sometimes he took local people straight from their homes, and burned and raided local towns. He then sailed across the Atlantic and sold the people as slaves in Spanish colonies in the West

Indies. These trips made John Hawkins rich. They also proved that selling human beings was a way to make huge amounts of money.

Hawkins had the backing of Queen Elizabeth I herself. She gave him money and ships to support his voyages, and rewarded his success at slave trading by making him a knight. The last voyage John Hawkins made, in 1568, was a failure. He lost three ships in a battle against the Spanish. For decades, the English gave up on the slave trade across the Atlantic.

Sir Francis Drake

To see what Africa meant to the Tudors, we can look at a man whose story has been told many times before. The most famous sea captain of Tudor times, Sir Francis Drake, is known as an English hero. As well as being the first person to captain a voyage all the way around the world, he helped to defeat the Spanish Armada's attack on England in 1588, and was knighted by Elizabeth I. He was also a cousin of the slave trader John Hawkins, and occasionally a slave trader himself. On one voyage, he worked with a group of Africans in central America called the Cimaroons, who helped him to capture Spanish silver. Some of the Cimaroons chose to join Drake's crew and sail back to England with him. One of them, whose name was Diego, was one of four African sailors who joined Drake on his historic journey around the world in 1577.

Elizabeth I gave Francis Drake a present which shows how important she thought his links with Africa were. The 'Drake Jewel' has a miniature portrait of Elizabeth on the inside, and on the outside a carved picture of a Black African man's head, in front of the head of a white European. The African's face could have been included to represent Drake's friends the Cimaroons. The jewel shows that for Tudor England, Africa was a land of opportunity. England wanted to use its ships to become a great power in the world, and Africa was part of that plan.

STUARTS

1603–1714

In 1603 James VI of Scotland also became King James I of England, and now ruled over both kingdoms. The Stuart period lasted for more than a hundred years, during which dramatic events shook Britain: a terrorist attack on Parliament, civil wars, plague, the Great Fire of London. One king was executed, and another was kicked out and replaced. Meanwhile, a story was unfolding which would change the world and re-draw Britain's relationship with people from Africa. Together with the Stuart royals, English merchants were developing new and brutal ways of making money. They built up slave-powered colonies in America and the West Indies and grew a trade in human beings that would make England the world's biggest slave-trading country.

When one country starts a new settlement in another place, run as part of the home country, it is called a 'colony'. Other European countries, like England's rival, Spain, already had colonies in the 'New World' on the other side of the Atlantic Ocean. In the seventeenth century, England began to join them by taking control of land in America and the Caribbean. These colonies would become places where millions of Africans were taken and forced to work in inhuman conditions.

These colonies would become places where millions of Africans were taken

The first successful British colony in North America was Jamestown in Virginia, where English settlers arrived in 1607. In a few years, farmers in Virginia found they could make money by growing tobacco to send back for sale in England. In the Caribbean, the first successful colony was the island of Barbados. There, the English settlers who arrived in 1627 found over time that one particular product could make them big profits: sugar.

The sugar cane plant grew well in Barbados, and people back in England loved its sweetness. The problem was that it took a lot of work to grow sugar cane and turn it into sugar ready to sell. After growing and harvesting the plants, the cane had to be processed quickly before it went off. Workers had to take the cane straight from the fields to squeeze the juice out of it between heavy rollers, and then get the juice quickly to the 'boiling house' to boil it down into raw sugar. This was hard, hot, dangerous work.

At first, the people doing this work on Barbados were mostly 'indentured servants' from England, Scotland, Ireland, and other parts of Europe. These were poor people and prisoners who were signed up to work for a period of seven to nine years. They were often very badly treated, but once their time was up they were free again.

Cutting sugar cane on a French plantation.

As the sugar trade grew, the landowners needed more workers than they could get from Europe, and they began to use more slaves from Africa. The English turned the land into bigger and bigger farms, using more and more slaves to produce more and more valuable sugar. In the middle of the seventeenth century, Barbados became a whole island dedicated to farming sugar on big farms called 'plantations', powered by the forced work of tens of thousands of enslaved people from Africa.

Soon there were more enslaved Africans than Europeans living on Barbados. To force the Africans to work and stop them rebelling, the English landowners wrote laws which set the rules for a new kind of slave society. In 1661 they wrote a set of laws called the 'Barbados Slave Code'.

The Barbados Slave Code

The Barbados Slave Code set out the system in which Africans lived as slaves on the island. An enslaved person remained an enslaved person for their whole life, and their children would automatically be enslaved too.

Enslaved people were not allowed weapons. Violent punishments were listed in the Code, which were much worse for enslaved Africans than for Europeans. A European who owned an enslaved person could hurt and even kill them without being punished. The law was totally different for Africans and Europeans on Barbados: a 'Christian' (white person) who was accused of a crime had the right to a trial by jury, but a Black person did not. To explain this unfairness, the slave codes said that Africans were different because they weren't Christian.

People from Britain and Europe weren't used to thinking of themselves as part of a group called 'white'

In this way, the strange new slave society split people by law into two clear groups: enslaved Black people, and white free people. It was around this time that the English started to use the word 'white' to talk about themselves. Before this, people from Britain and Europe weren't used to thinking of themselves as part of a group called 'white'. The landowners in the West Indies hoped that if poor Europeans saw themselves as white like their rulers, not

Black like other workers, they would be more likely to support the rulers if the Black slaves rebelled.

The slave system of Barbados spread to the other colonies which England began in the West Indies, like the much bigger island of Jamaica. These systems also shaped laws in the English colonies in North America, where tobacco instead of sugar was the main crop farmed by slaves.

Using enslaved people to grow sugar on West Indian plantations was a separate business from buying and selling people as slaves. Before about 1650, only a few English ships brought people from Africa to be slaves. Instead, the English colonists mostly used enslaved people stolen or bought from foreign traders. What changed this was the arrival in 1660 of a new King of England: Charles II.

Charles saw an opportunity to make money by trading in enslaved people. English ships would take people from

The coat of arms of the Royal African Company, with its emblem of an elephant and castle.

Africa to be slaves in the English colonies. Together with his brother James, Duke of York (the future King James II), King Charles gave his support and money to companies which were set up to trade in enslaved people. The company he set up in 1672, the Royal African Company, would be the only one allowed to trade all along the western coast of Africa. Any other English merchants caught breaking this rule could have their ships taken by the Royal Navy. The Duke of York himself ran the company as its Governor. This powerful, royal-led business enslaved more people than any other British company in history. Around 150,000 African people were taken across the Atlantic into slavery by the Royal African Company alone.

> This powerful, royal-led business enslaved more people than any other British company in history

Like other European slave traders, the Royal African Company built forts called 'slave castles' around the coast of West Africa. The traders lived comfortably in the slave castles, with good food and plenty of wine. In other parts of the castles, the people they had bought from local slave traders were kept prisoner. Some traders burned the initials RAC (Royal African Company) or DY (Duke of York) permanently into the enslaved people's skin to mark them as the company's property. Iron shackles were fixed around their legs so they could be chained up. They were then loaded onto overcrowded ships for the horrific journey across the Atlantic Ocean, known as the 'Middle Passage'. Around one-fifth of the enslaved people on these Royal African Company ships died before they even reached the other side.

The Royal African Company put Britain on the path to becoming the biggest slave-trading country in Europe. After King James II's rule ended, other companies fought to be allowed to buy and sell slaves as well. They made it even busier and even more profitable. In all, British traders enslaved over three million people. Over the next century, the money which British companies made from taking Africans across the ocean to be slaves flowed back into the country and paid for grand buildings, businesses, industries and wealthy families all over Britain.

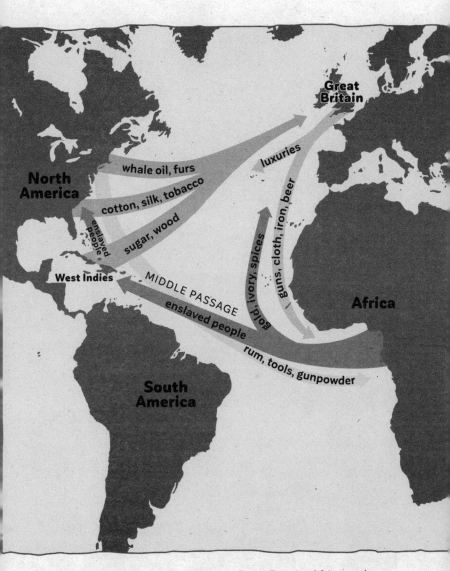

The triangle of trade between Great Britain, Africa and the American colonies.

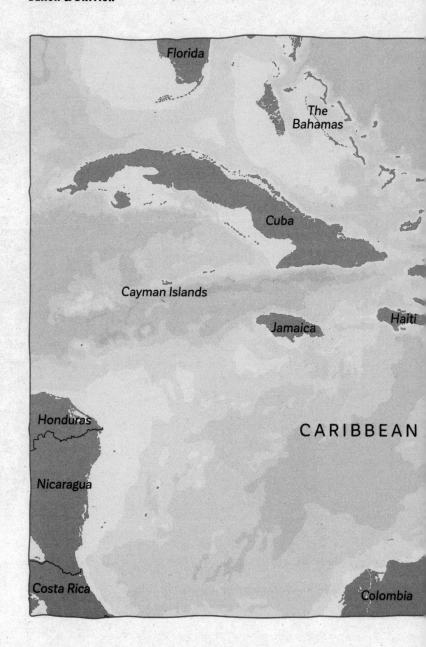

Florida

The
Bahamas

Cuba

Cayman Islands

Jamaica

Haiti

CARIBBEAN

Honduras

Nicaragua

Costa Rica

Colombia

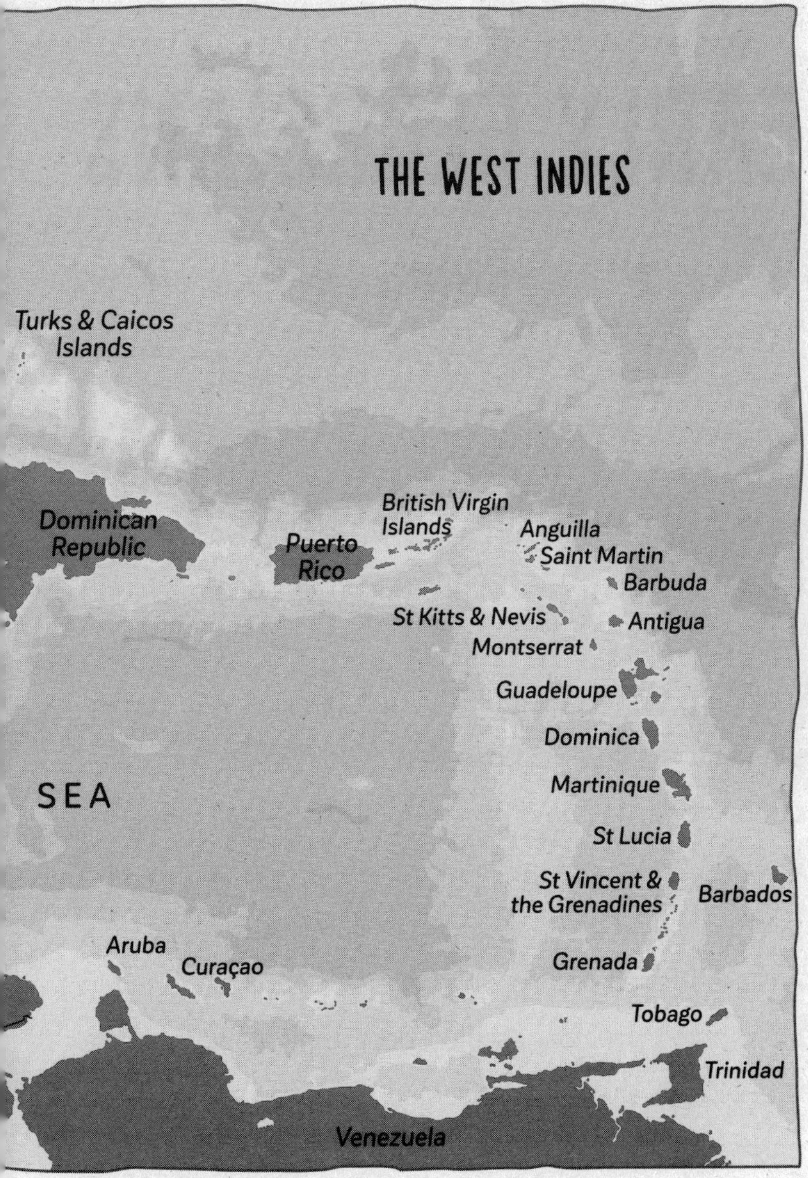

THE WEST INDIES

Turks & Caicos
Islands

Dominican
Republic

Puerto
Rico

British Virgin
Islands

Anguilla

Saint Martin

Barbuda

St Kitts & Nevis

Antigua

Montserrat

Guadeloupe

Dominica

SEA

Martinique

St Lucia

St Vincent &
the Grenadines

Barbados

Aruba

Curaçao

Grenada

Tobago

Trinidad

Venezuela

EARLY GEORGIANS

1714–1776

In the early eighteenth century the Hanoverian kings came to the throne. By then Britain's colonies in North America and on the islands of the West Indies were making huge fortunes for the rich families who owned plantations there. On those plantations were grown sugar, cotton, tobacco and other products that would only grow in warm and sunny parts of the world. The people who did the work of planting and harvesting those crops were enslaved Black people who were brought from Africa in slave ships. Thousands died on the plantations where they were overworked, neglected, not given enough food and beaten. The same ships that carried the slaves to the colonies were later filled with sugar and other crops, and sailed back to Britain.

The captains of the slave ships were able to make extra money by bringing one or two enslaved Black people back to Britain with them on the last leg of their journeys.

These enslaved people were bought by rich families who made them work for them as servants. When they were no longer wanted they were advertised for sale in the newspapers. Here are some of those advertisements:

To be S O L D,

A Negroe Servant about Seventeen Years of Age, born on the Gold Coast, from which Place he was brought five Years since. He is about five Foot four Inches high, well made, and very streight; speaks English well, and understands the Business of a Family Footman. Any Person wanting such a Servant, may be further informed by applying to the Universal Register Office, opposite Cecil-Street in the Strand.

To be Sold,

A healthy NEGRO SLAVE,

Named PRINCE,

Seventeen Years of Age, five Feet ten Inches high, and extremely well-grown,

Enquire on JOSHUA SPRINGER, in St. Stephen's-Lane.

We will never know how many Black people were brought to Britain in those years, but we can learn more about them through art because in hundreds of paintings from the Georgian period you can see the faces of Black people who were brought to Britain. You can find them in paintings by famous artists like Joshua Reynolds, Johan Zoffany and William Hogarth, especially in portraits. The rich had portraits painted so that they could show off their wealth – their fine clothes, jewellery, horses and beautiful houses. Those who owned enslaved Black people sometimes included them in their portraits, having them sitting or standing alongside them. They did this because owning enslaved Black people was fashionable; they were keen to show off their human property.

> Owning enslaved Black people was fashionable; they were keen to show off their human property.

What we can tell from these portraits, and from other clues, is that many of the Black people brought to Britain as slaves were very young. Most of them were young

*The 3rd Duke of Richmond is depicted out on a shoot with a
Black boy in fine livery, c. 1765 in this painting by Zoffany.*

boys. One enslaved boy named Scipio Africanus, who
was made to work for Charles William Howard, the 7th
Earl of Suffolk, was just eighteen when he died in 1720.
His grave is in a churchyard in Bristol. There were some
enslaved girls and women, but they were less valuable
and fewer of them were brought to Britain by slave-ship
captains. To make these enslaved children appear even

more fashionable, they were dressed in expensive and colourful uniforms with metal buttons and neat jackets, which we can see in the portraits. Because these Black people were the property of the rich people who paid for the portraits to be painted, they were usually placed in the margins of the painting, sometimes pushed up against the frame. They were also painted looking at their rich owners and sometimes holding exotic fruits from Africa or Asia, monkeys, parrots or rare birds.

There is another place where we can learn about the lives of enslaved people in Georgian Britain. As they longed to be free, and because many were treated badly by the rich people who owned them, some attempted to escape. As enslaved Black people were very valuable, owners would pay for advertisements to be put in the newspapers offering rewards for their recapture. These were known as 'Hue and Cry' advertisements, and they tell us how old the enslaved people were, what they looked like, whether they were boys or men, girls or women, and they describe the colourful uniforms they were made to wear.

Here are some of those advertisements:

ELOPED,

The 5th of FEBRUARY, 1763, from JOHN STONE, Efq. of CHIPPENAAM,

A NEGRO SERVANT,

Named GLOUCESTER;

Twenty-one Years of Age, about five Feet fix Inches high, flender grown, marked with a long Scar down the Middle of his Forehead, and fpeaks Englifh tolerably well. Wore, when he went off, a light-coloured Cloth Livery Coat, and red Waiftcoat, with white Metal Buttons; the Coat with a Red turned-down Collar, red Button-Holes, red Lining, and Slafh Sleeves. Had on likewife a black Velvet Cap, with a Silver Band, or elfe a Silver laced Hat, and an old Pair of Leather Breeches.

Whoever fecures the faid Negro, and gives Notice of it to JOHN STONE, Efq. aforefaid, fo that he may be brought back again, will be fufficiently rewarded for their Trouble.—But any Perfon countenancing or harbouring the faid Black, will be profecuted agreeable to Law.

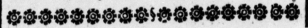

RUN away from his Mafter on the 2d Inftant, David Marat, a Black about feventeen Years of Age, with fhort wooly Hair; He had on a whitifh Cloath Livery, Lin'd with Blew, and Princes-mettal Buttons, with a Turbant on his Head: He founds a Trumpet, whoever fecures him and brings him to Edward Talbot Efq; by Kingftreet near Soho, fhall have five Guines Reward.

> **E**LOPED from Mr. SAMUEL
> DELPRATT, Merchant, at Briftol, and come
> to London, A NEGRO MAN, about 17 or 18 Years
> old, Five Feet Five or Six Inches high, had on when
> he left Briftol, a brown Livery Coat lined with Red,
> red Button Holes and Collar, red Waiftcoat, a Pair of
> old Leather Breeches pieced at the Knee, a black
> Leather Cap, and a Pair of black ribbed Stockings,
> anfwers to the Name of JOHN; if he fhould offer to
> fhip himfelf as a free Man, on Board any Ship, by
> directing a Line to the Jamaica Coffee Houfe, for
> Capt. William Tomlinfon, or to Mr. Jofeph Malpas,
> Jeweller, in Wood Street, Cheapfide, whatever Ex-
> pence in ftopping the faid Negro fhall be repaid with
> Thanks, and Six Guineas Reward.

These enslaved Black people were also given classical names such as Caesar, Scipio and Pompey. They were not allowed to use their real African names. Some had been born on plantations in the British colonies and were brought to Britain by plantation owners rather than slave-ship captains. As well as expensive and fashionable uniforms some enslaved people in Georgian Britain were forced to wear slave collars. These strips of metal were attached around their necks and padlocked so they could not be removed. They were used to make it clear to everyone that the Black person wearing them was a slave and someone's property. Some slave collars had the initials or the name of the slave owner engraved into them. Visitors from abroad who came to London in those years sometimes wrote letters home describing the numbers of enslaved Black people they saw working for the rich. When the Russian Tsarina decided she wanted to buy Black slaves to work as servants in her court, she sent her agents to London. They were instructed to buy a 'number of the finest best made black boys in order to be sent to Petersburg as attendants on Her Russian Majesty'.

The true number of Black people living in Britain in the Georgian period is a mystery that historians will never be able to solve. What we do know is that not all Black people were enslaved. There were also free Black people, some of whom were former slaves who had been freed, and others escaped slaves who lived in fear of being kidnapped by slave catchers and sent to the plantations

> The true number of Black people in Britain in the Georgian period is a mystery ... we do know that not all Black people were enslaved.

in Jamaica or Barbados. Even free Black people were at risk of being kidnapped and sent to work as slaves in the West Indies.

Among the free Black population were Black sailors. We know because we have the records of the ships that fought in big naval battles, like the Battle of Trafalgar in 1805. On the ships that the British Admiral Horatio Nelson led into battle against the French and the Spanish fleets at Trafalgar were eighteen men who had been born in Africa and another 123 who were from the West Indies. There was an African sailor and six sailors from the islands of the West Indies serving on Nelson's flagship HMS *Victory*.

> Among the free Black population were Black sailors.

Among the Africans at Trafalgar were George Brown, who had been born in Guinea in Africa and was just thirteen at the time of the Battle, and John Amboyne, who was twenty-seven years old and had also been born in Guinea. Another African called John Ephraim served on board

HMS *Temeraire*. He had been born on Africa's Calabar Coast, in what is today Nigeria.

The role of the Black sailors was remembered in the years after the battle. At the base of Nelson's Column in Trafalgar Square in London are four huge bronze panels. One of them, called 'The Death of Nelson', shows the moment just after Admiral Nelson has been shot by a French sniper. Beside Nelson and the other officers is a Black sailor holding a musket.

A few of the free Black people who lived in Britain in the eighteenth century wrote books about their lives. They were the lucky few who had been taught how to read and write. One of them was Ignatius Sancho, who had been born on board a slave ship in 1729. He was brought up in Greenwich by three wealthy sisters who did not think it was right for a Black child to be taught to read and write. However, the young Sancho set out to educate himself, and was helped to do so by the Duke and Duchess of Montague who lived nearby. They gave him books, and

eventually he went to work for them as a butler. When the duke and duchess died, they left Sancho some money, and he became a shopkeeper in London with his wife Anne, a free Black woman. Sancho spent his time writing and became friends with some famous writers and actors. He had his portrait painted by the famous artist Thomas Gainsborough.

Another fortunate Black Georgian was Julius Soubise, who was born into slavery on the Caribbean island of St Kitts. Brought to Britain by a captain in the Royal Navy, he was sold to Catherine Hyde, the Duchess of Queensberry, a rich and eccentric woman. The duchess treated Soubise well, educated him, and by the time he was a teenager Soubise was both an expert swordsman and skilled at riding horses. As a young man he became a playboy,

A satirical cartoon from the late eighteenth century showing Julius Soubise fencing with his patron Catherine Hyde, the Duchess of Queensbury.

partying in Georgian London with his famous friends and becoming an amateur actor, musician and poet. The duchess paid the bills for his lavish lifestyle. After a scandal he was sent to live in India, where he became a horse-riding instructor. He died in 1798 after being thrown from a horse.

Ignatius Sancho and Julius Soubise were educated and protected by members of the wealthy aristocracy. This allowed them to live their lives in some comfort, often alongside the rich and famous. Other Black Georgians were far less fortunate. James Albert Ukawsaw Gronniosaw was born in Nigeria but captured and sold into slavery. Ukawsaw had been taught to read in America, by the man who owned him. When he was given his freedom he became a soldier in the British Army in America before moving to Britain, where he met his wife Elizabeth. As Ukawsaw and Elizabeth and their children had little money, they struggled to survive and sometimes did not have enough food to eat. A book about his life was published after his death.

The life of Nathaniel Wells couldn't have been more different. His father was a white plantation owner on the Caribbean island of St Kitts, and his mother an enslaved woman. Wells was sent to London in 1794 for an education, but when his father died he inherited a huge fortune. As well as money, this inheritance included three sugar estates and hundreds of enslaved people, including his own mother. Under the law, Nathaniel was now his mother's owner. He freed his mother and a handful of other relatives who were also enslaved, but he did not free the others. Despite being mixed-race he continued to own slaves. Nathaniel used his fortune to buy a big house in the countryside in Wales and became a country gentleman, living a comfortable life. He became a magistrate, judging people brought to court. He never returned to St Kitts, and managed his estates from Wales.

Was slavery legal in Britain?

Although there were both enslaved and free Black people in Georgian Britain, there was one simple question that no one had the answer to – was slavery legal in Britain or not? In the colonies in North America and the West Indies, laws had been created to make slavery legal and to allow the owners of slaves to inflict terrible punishments on enslaved people. Those laws, like the Barbados Slave Code, stated that Africans were items of property, just like animals, land or houses. Those same laws stated that the children born to an enslaved mother automatically became slaves and made it very difficult for Black people to become free. But there were no laws for slavery in Britain itself, and what no one knew was

Should judges in Britain see Black people who had been slaves in the colonies as people, or as items of property?

whether an enslaved person coming to England, Wales or Scotland remained a slave or if they had the same rights to be protected by the law as any white person. Should judges in Britain see Black people who had been slaves in the colonies as people, or as items of property? The judges themselves could not agree, and over the years different conflicting opinions had been put forward. Many Black people believed they would be free the moment they settled on British soil. Or that they could no longer be a slave if they were baptized and became Christians.

Jonathan Strong

One day in the winter of 1765 a lawyer from Barbados named David Lisle savagely beat an enslaved boy called Jonathan Strong who lived with him in his house in London. He struck the boy on the head and face with a pistol then threw him into the street. We do not know exactly how old Jonathan Strong was, but he was probably a teenager. Somehow he survived and found his way to a street called Mincing Lane in the City of London, where William Sharp, a famous doctor, had his surgery. Once a week Dr Sharp opened his doors to the poor. While in the queue waiting to be seen, Jonathan Strong was spotted by the doctor's younger brother, Granville Sharp, who rushed him in to the surgery. 'The boy seemed ready to die,' Granville Sharp later said. The two Sharp brothers sent him to hospital and paid for his care. When he was better they found him a job. For the

Granville Sharp dedicated fifty years of his life
to campaigning against slavery.

first time in his life Strong was no longer a slave and had some money of his own. Two years later David Lisle saw him in the street, and arranged for him to be kidnapped. Lisle then sold him for £30 to a man called James Kerr, who owned a plantation in Jamaica. Kerr planned to send Strong to Jamaica to work as a slave. But Strong, who had learned to read and write, sent a message to Granville Sharp, who came to his aid. Sharp succeeded in persuading the Lord Mayor to release Jonathan Strong. James Kerr then tried to take Granville Sharp to court in order to force him to release Strong. But Sharpe began to study the law and became so knowledgeable that he was able to force Kerr to give up trying to have Strong handed over to him.

Strong was a free man, but Granville Sharp kept studying the law. Sharp wrote a book on slavery and the law. Like many books in the eighteenth century, it had a very long title – *A Representation of the Injustice and Dangerous Tendency of Tolerating Slavery, or of Admitting the Least Claim of Private Property in the Persons of Men, in England.*

What he discovered was that the Black people in Georgian London lived in fear of kidnappers and slave catchers. So, from 1765 to 1772, Sharp looked out for a case that might be brought to court that would force the judges to make up their mind and decide if slavery was legal, or if the thousands of people kept as slaves in England were in reality free people.

The case that Granville Sharp was waiting for arrived one day in 1772 when a man called James Somerset came to Sharp's house looking for help. He had been brought to London from Virginia three years earlier by the man who had owned him for twenty years, Charles Stewart. In London, Somerset began to notice the numbers of free Black people. He may well have begun to think that perhaps he could escape and hide from Stewart in such a big city. He might also have come to believe that Stewart had no right to keep him as a slave, because in 1771 Somerset had been baptized and welcomed into the Church. Whatever his reasons, after two years in London, James Somerset escaped.

Charles Stewart hired slave-hunters, and two months later, James was kidnapped and taken to a ship on the Thames. There he was put in chains and taken down into the dark of the lower decks. Now he had his property back, Charles Stewart decided to send James to Jamaica to work as a slave on the sugar plantations. But James was saved by people from his church who had him released, and with Granville Sharp's help he took his case to court.

What Granville Sharp wanted to do was to use the case of James Somerset to prove that slavery was not legal in Britain. Charles Stewart and his lawyers tried to prove that it was. The court case was

Sharp wanted to prove that slavery was not legal in Britain

reported in all the newspapers and everyone awaited a final decision.

The man whose job it was to deliver that decision was the judge – Lord Mansfield. He tried very hard to not have to reach a ruling. At the end of the court case he went home to his mansion, Kenwood House, to think.

Living with Lord Mansfield at Kenwood House was a young woman named Dido Elizabeth Belle. She was the daughter of Lord Mansfield's nephew but her mother had been an enslaved African woman named Maria. In 1765, when she was just four years old, she was brought to England and put under the care of Lord Mansfield and his wife Elizabeth Murray. She was brought up at Kenwood House alongside another girl, Elizabeth, whose parents had died. Dido was treated affectionately but not as an equal; she did work around the house. So as Lord Mansfield was making his historic decision about slavery in England, he was sharing his home with his mixed-race grand-niece, a girl he had cared for for most of her life.

Lord Mansfield delivered his judgement in Westminster Hall in London on Monday, 22 June 1772. The hall was crowded with members of the public, reporters from the newspapers, and the supporters of the slave owners. Also present were a number of Black Georgians, the people who lived their lives in fear of being kidnapped and sold into slavery. Lord Mansfield's decision, when it came, was that

Charles Stewart did not have the right under English law to seize James Somerset on English soil and deport him to the colonies. Therefore James Somerset was a free man.

A newspaper called the *Public Advertiser* reported that after the decision 'two hundred blacks with their ladies had an entertainment at a public-house in Westminster, to celebrate the triumph which their brother Somerset had obtained over Mr. Stuart, his master. Lord Mansfield's health was echoed around the room; and the evening was concluded with a ball.'

In 1772 Joseph Knight, an enslaved African man living in Scotland, heard about the Somerset case and Lord Mansfield's decision. Joseph Knight had been born in Africa, captured by slave traders and sold in Jamaica to a man called John Wedderburn. In 1769 Wedderburn had taken Knight to Scotland with him. When he learned about Lord Mansfield's decision, Knight believed that it meant that he too was a free man, even though Scotland had its own separate laws and legal system. He demanded that John Wedderburn pay him wages for his work. When Wedderburn refused, Joseph Knight left and began to live life as a free man. But he was later arrested by John Wedderburn. When Joseph Knight's case went to court in 1774 the court decided that Knight had to return to Wedderburn and work for him for no wages. But Joseph Knight took his case to a higher court and the decision was overruled. In 1777 another appeal confirmed that slavery was not recognised under Scots Law and that Joseph Knight was a free man.

On 17 April 1773 Granville Sharp recorded in his diary that 'Poor Jonathan Strong, the first Negro whose freedom I had procured in 1767, died this morning.' Jonathan Strong was only around twenty-five years old. He had never fully recovered from the vicious beating he had suffered at the hands of David Lisle in 1765.

LATE GEORGIANS

1777–1837

By the 1770s there were half a million people living as slaves in Britain's colonies in North America. That means that around one in five of the people in those colonies were enslaved Africans. Tensions between the white population of the colonies and the British government over tax and other issues led some to rebel against British rule. They became known as the American Patriots. In 1775, when rebellion broke out in Virginia, the largest of the North American colonies, the man in charge was British Governor John Murray, the 4th Earl of Dunmore.

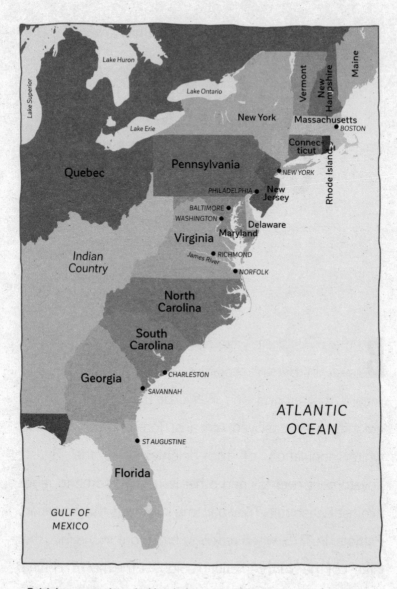

British possessions in North America, 1775, before the war began.

To fight the Patriots he based himself and his forces on a fleet of around a hundred British ships on the James River. In 1775 Dunmore wrote a proclamation that was printed and then sent across Virginia. It promised that if slaves whose owners had joined the rebellion escaped and came to the British forces on the James River, and if they agreed to fight against the Patriots, they would be given their freedom. Within two weeks hundreds of enslaved people had left their masters and made their way to Dunmore's forces on the James River. Some managed to reach the British ships in small boats, others waded through the swamps and then swam to the ships.

On board they were formed into a new regiment: Dunmore's Royal Ethiopian Regiment. They were given guns and new uniforms, and on those uniforms was sewn a badge that read 'Liberty to Slaves'. Freedom was on offer only to enslaved people whose owners were Patriots, and only to those who were willing to fight for the British.

Freedom was on offer only to enslaved people who were willing to fight for the British

This meant women and children could not win their freedom this way.

By the end of 1775 there were 300 Black men in the Ethiopian Regiment. In 1776 the American Patriots declared their independence from Britain, creating a new country, the United States of America. But the British kept fighting as they were determined to keep hold of their colonies and end the revolution. By then, enough former slaves had joined the British forces that a second regiment, the Black Pioneers, was created.

Between 1775 and 1781 the former slaves fought for the British against the Americans. Some became spies behind enemy lines, others worked as labourers, blacksmiths, woodcutters, tailors, nurses and officers' servants. They dug trenches and prepared defences, they built the camps in which the armies were billeted. The American Patriots also had Black men fighting against the British in their army and navy.

In 1779 the British General Sir Henry Clinton, who was in charge of British forces in North America, wrote another proclamation. He promised freedom to all slaves whose masters had joined the Patriots. All they had to do was come over to the British side. They did not have to join the British forces. This meant that enslaved women and children were now able to win their freedom as well as men. Enslaved people who were the property of George Washington, the American general who later became the first president of the United States of America, escaped to join the British, as did Black men and women who were owned by Thomas Jefferson, the man who wrote America's Declaration of Independence and who became America's third president. Over the course of the war perhaps as many as 100,000 enslaved people escaped and came over to the British.

> Perhaps as many as 100,000 enslaved people escaped and came over to the British

By 1781 the British forces were losing the war in North America. The British army became surrounded by an American army led by George

Washington at a place called Yorktown. Washington was being helped by the French – the old enemies of the British. After the British were forced to surrender negotiations began to bring the war to an end and arrange for the British forces to leave the United States of America.

The Black people who had escaped from their owners and come over to the British knew that if they stayed in the United States they would be recaptured and enslaved again. Some went to New York, one of the cities the British still controlled. Among them was a former slave called Harry Washington. Harry's former owner, George Washington, was determined to recapture all the slaves who had escaped from his plantation. He had a list of their names and planned to find them, once his American army had captured New York.

George Washington was determined to recapture all the slaves who had escaped from his plantation

In 1783 the British army officers in America decided that anyone who did not want to remain in the United States would be helped to leave. White people and the slaves they owned, along with the free Black people who had joined the British during the war, were put on ships that set sail from the ports of Savannah in Georgia, Charleston in South Carolina, and New York harbour. On 25 November 1783 George Washington marched his army into New York. At 1 p.m. a cannon was fired to signal that the last of the British soldiers had left the city. The war was over. George Washington did not find his former slave Harry Washington in New York: Harry was among the 3,000 Black people who had left on British ships. Most of those former slaves were sent to Nova Scotia in British-controlled Canada, but some were brought to Britain.

The Black people who had joined the British during the American Revolution were fortunate to have escaped from slavery, but they had no friends or families in Britain. A few got help from the government but most had no money and were left homeless. They were unable to find jobs and had to sleep on the streets of

London. They became known as the Black Poor, and to help them a group of rich businessmen collected money and used it to buy food and winter clothes. With no homes and no jobs, some of the former slaves wanted the government to send them to another country, where they could be given land to farm and grow food. Some wanted to be sent to Nova Scotia, where most of the other former slaves from North America had been settled. But instead it was decided to send the Black Poor to Sierra Leone on the coast of West Africa.

There the government would buy land from the local African king and give that land to the Black Poor to create a new settlement. Preparations were made, and Granville Sharp, the man who had helped Jonathan Strong and James Somerset, gave his support. Sharp encouraged the Black Poor to agree to start new lives in Sierra Leone and he called the new settlement the Province of Freedom. The government provided ships and money to buy equipment.

In 1787, three years after the Black Poor had been evacuated from New York, three ships – the *Belisarius*, the *Atlantic* and the *Vernon* – set sail for the coast of Sierra Leone. On board were 456 people. They were not just Black people who had been evacuated from America, but also other Black Londoners who had escaped from slave owners, and found themselves living on the streets of that city. There were also a number of white women who had married Black men who had joined the expedition with their husbands and their mixed-race children.

They arrived in Sierra Leone after a month at sea. They built huts to live in and began to plough the land and plant crops. The site chosen for this new settlement, a place that was now home to hundreds of former slaves, was near one of the centres of the slave trade. And as they built their new home, slave ships passed by on the Sierra Leone River, their holds packed with other Africans, chained together and being sent to the plantations of America and the West Indies.

Just two weeks after they had arrived, Sierra Leone's rainy season began. The rain was so heavy that it washed away the crops the settlers had planted. Then insects emerged that began to eat the crops that had survived. Water rushed down from the mountains, and strong winds damaged the huts the settlers had built, and ripped apart the tents they had brought with them from London. The settlers began to fall ill with tropical diseases like malaria.

There was an outbreak of dysentery and some of the settlers began to die. By September 1788 only 130 of the original settlers were left alive. Eventually, the land on which the settlement had been built was seized by one of the local African kings, and the last of the settlers were driven out. The whole project had been a disastrous failure and most of the Black settlers had died.

Granville Sharp was shocked by the suffering of the Black Poor and the failure of the Province of Freedom. He and his supporters in London raised money to send a second wave of colonists to Sierra Leone in 1792. This time they

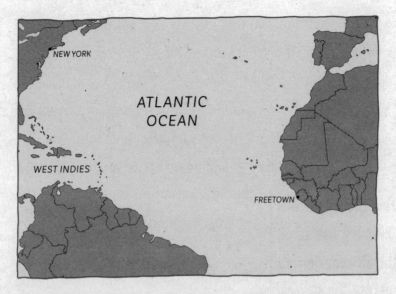

The journey from New York to Sierra Leone took a month.

came from among the Black settlers who had been sent from New York to Nova Scotia, and among them was Harry Washington. The new settlement was called Freetown. As they settled down to work, the new settlers created a new community. They held regular meetings called 'palavers' under the shade of a huge cotton silk tree. Although many of them died of disease, and although life in Freetown was extremely difficult, the settlers were able to create a new community, and Freetown today is a big city, the capital of Sierra Leone.

Historians think the total number of people shipped to America and the West Indies by the British during the era of the Atlantic Slave Trade (1640-1807) was around 3.5 million. It took around 11,000 separate journeys by slave ships to carry that many people across the Atlantic. During the eighteenth century, half of all the Africans carried across the Atlantic into slavery were transported by British ships.

During the eighteenth century, half of all the Africans carried across the Atlantic into slavery were transported by British ships

The slave traders and those who made their living selling the tropical goods that the enslaved people produced made a huge amount of money, and their wealth transformed cities like Bristol, Liverpool and Glasgow. To most people in Britain it seemed that slavery was so important to the economy of Britain that it could never be brought to an end. The country was also addicted to the products the slaves produced, most important of which was sugar. At the time of the Tudors sugar had been a luxury that only the very richest people could afford. Using enslaved people to grow it on plantations in the West Indies made it much cheaper, and sugar became part of most people's diets. By the early nineteenth century only the very poorest people in Britain could not afford sugar.

Lots of people also relied on slavery and the slave trade for jobs. They worked on slave ships or worked making goods that were sent to Africa and exchanged for enslaved people. Or they made the chains and shackles that were attached to the enslaved people, or they worked building the slave ships themselves. Other people worked processing the sugar that was brought back from the West Indies, or the tobacco and cotton that were also produced using slave labour. Money from slavery was everywhere, and the products produced by enslaved people were part of the daily lives of millions of people.

When some people criticized slavery, the slave owners justified it by claiming that Africans were inferior to white people. They said Africans were naturally savage and that slavery was the best way of controlling them and making them useful. Many of the racist ideas that still exist today were invented by the slave owners and their supporters in the eighteenth century.

But many people accepted slavery because they knew very little about it. Although there were thousands of Black people living in Britain in the eighteenth century, the plantations of the West Indies were thousands of miles away and most people didn't know what conditions were like there or on the slave ships. The suffering of Africans was hidden from view.

People began to see slavery as a national shame. They wanted to see the slave trade abolished and then the slaves in the colonies set free

In the 1770s, however, more and more people began to see slavery as a national shame. They wanted to see the slave trade abolished and then the slaves already in the colonies set free. These people created what was called the 'Abolitionist Movement', and they became known as abolitionists. Their first job was to educate the public about the realities of slavery and the slave trade so that more people would understand why it needed to be abolished.

The formal Abolitionist Movement began on 22 May 1787, when twelve men gathered together at a printing shop at 2 George Yard in London. There they formed themselves into what they called the Society for Effecting the Abolition of the Slave Trade. They included Granville Sharp, the pottery entrepreneur Josiah Wedgwood, the Quaker banker and philanthropist Samuel Hoare, and Thomas Clarkson, who was to lead the movement, later alongside the prominent MP William Wilberforce. The early abolitionists focused upon the slave trade, rather than slavery. They concluded that the Middle Passage of the slave trade was the most deadly and inhumane aspect of slavery as it was then that an enslaved person suffered most greatly and faced the greatest risk of death. Many abolitionists also believed that if the slave trade were ended, the supply of slaves would be cut off and the slave owners would understand that the enslaved people could not be replaced and would decide to treat them better and improve their food and housing.

The abolitionists threw their energies into a campaign of public education. They wrote and published thousands of pamphlets and pioneered the use of the mass petition – these were huge lists that contained the signatures of thousands of people who wanted to let the government know that they were opposed to slavery. Between 1787 and 1792, 1.5 million people in Britain signed petitions against the slave trade, at a time when the national population of Britain was just 12 million. Much of the work organizing the abolitionist movement was done by women, who at the time did not have the right to vote in elections. Female abolitionists formed their own organizations and committees, and threw themselves into the campaign. Women abolitionists played a major role in promoting another of the tactics used by the abolitionist movement: boycotting of products produced by enslaved people. They urged people to refuse to buy or eat sugar that had been produced on plantations by the enslaved. Instead they urged people to buy sugar produced in India by free people, or to use lemon to flavour their tea.

The most dramatic part of the abolitionist movement was the organization of huge public meetings. Thousands of them were held across the country. At these meetings speakers came on stage and lectured the audience about the horrors of slavery. Sometimes the speeches went on for hours, and the best abolitionist speakers were celebrities, famous for the emotional power and passion of their speeches. At the end of the speeches the abolitionists encouraged the audience to sign their petitions and buy anti-slavery pamphlets and books.

Olaudah Equiano and Ottobah Cugoano

Two of the most important abolitionist books were written by Black abolitionists, Olaudah Equiano and Ottobah Cugoano. Cugoano's book was called *Thoughts and Sentiments on the Evil of Slavery and Commerce of the Human Species.* It told the story of his life. He had been born on the Gold Coast of Africa but kidnapped by slave-traders at around the age of thirteen. He was then enslaved on the island of Grenada and forced to work on sugar plantations until he was sold to a new owner who brought him to England. In 1773, after Lord Mansfield's decision had freed James Somerset, Cugoano left his owner and was baptized in London. As a free man he learned to read and write, and with the help of Olaudah Equiano wrote his book in which he described what he called the 'misery and cruelty' of slavery. Copies of Cugoano's shocking book were given to powerful people, including King George III.

Cugoano's friend Olaudah Equiano's book was published in 1789. It was called The Interesting Narrative of the Life of Olaudah Equiano. It was one of the best-selling books of the time. Equiano was born in what is now the country of Nigeria on the coast of West Africa, but when he was just a boy of eleven he was captured by African slave traders who sold him to Europeans. They took him on a slave ship to Barbados and then

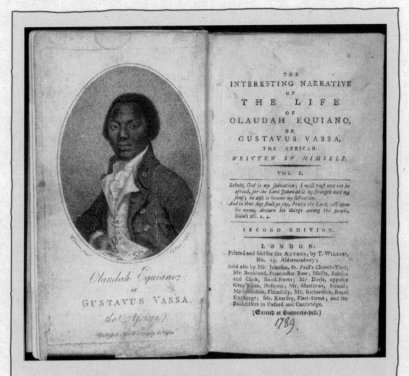

The title page of Olaudah Equiano's book.

Virginia. Equiano was not put to work on the plantations. Instead he worked on board the ships. For twenty years he worked as an enslaved sailor travelling across the West Indies, North America and Central America. In that time he was sold three times and owned by three different men. One of them decided to name him Gustavus Vassa, after a famous Swedish king. By the

1780s Equiano was a free man living in London. He had purchased his own freedom with money he earned trading goods between the different islands of the West Indies. By 1783 Equiano had become involved in the early abolitionist movement and had got to know Granville Sharp. His book made him a celebrity and he used his fame to bring crowds to abolitionist meetings.

Olaudah Equiano and Ottobah Cugoano formed the Sons of Africa, a group of Black Britons who had either been slaves or who were the children of enslaved parents. They were the Black abolitionists, and they included Boughwa Gegansmel, Jasper Goree, Cojoh Ammere, George Robert Mandeville, Thomas Jones, William Stevens, Joseph Almze, John Christopher, James Bailey, Thomas Oxford and George Wallace. The Sons of Africa were just as energetic as the white abolitionists, writing letters and making speeches. Sadly, the records of their activities are incomplete and there is much about them that remains unknown. As well as the Sons of Africa, other Black Britons took part in the struggles against the trade and slavery. They included Phillis Wheatley, James Gronniosaw, Ignatius Sancho and later Mary Prince.

The enormous task the abolitionists faced was to educate the public about the realities of the slave trade and slavery. Which is why the voices of Black abolitionists who had themselves been enslaved were among the most powerful. At their huge meetings some abolitionist speakers showed people the manacles, shackles, metal punishment collars and whips used by the slave traders. To make people realize how horrific the slave trade was, the abolitionists also reminded the public of a terrible event that had taken place in 1781.

> The voices of Black abolitionists who had themselves been enslaved were among the most powerful

That year a British slave ship called the Zong had set sail from Accra on the coast of West Africa and headed across the Atlantic to Jamaica in the West Indies. It was carrying 442 captives, around twice the number a ship of that size was supposed to have on board. The owners of the *Zong* were a group of Liverpool businessmen and they took out insurance on the lives of the captives on board. This meant that if they died during the journey the owners would receive compensation from the insurance company. It was entirely normal for businessmen to insure the cargo of a ship. It made no difference to the owners of the *Zong* that the cargo their ship was carrying was human beings.

During the journey the crew of the *Zong* made several mistakes navigating to Jamaica. This meant that there was a risk that the ship would run out of fresh drinking water. Disease had broken out among the enslaved people in the hold and among the crew. The crew wanted to make sure that some of the slaves survived and reached Jamaica alive so they could be sold for a profit. The captain of the *Zong* told the crew that the insurance company would not pay money for the loss of any slaves who died of disease but, if the sick slaves were thrown overboard, the insurance money could be claimed. So, over three days, the crew threw 133 of the most unwell of the enslaved people overboard into the ocean, where they drowned. By the time the *Zong* arrived in Jamaica only 208 of the 442 Africans who had been put on board in Accra were still alive.

When the Liverpool businessman who owned the *Zong* tried to claim insurance on the people who had been thrown overboard the insurance company refused to pay and in 1783 the case was taken to court. Olaudah Equiano heard about what had happened on the *Zong* and he told Granville Sharp, who tried but failed to have the surviving crew members of the *Zong* convicted of murder. When this was unsuccessful Sharp wrote and published an account of the *Zong* massacre that shocked public opinion. What people came to understand was that the murder of the sick or rebellious captives on board slave ships was normal practice.

> The murder of sick or rebellious captives on board slave ships was normal practice

The darkest and most terrible secrets of the slave trade were being revealed to the public.

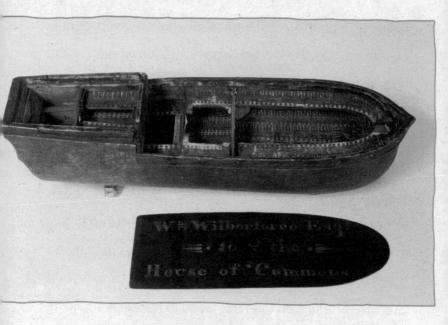

A model of the slave ship Brooks *that was commissioned by abolitionist Thomas Clarkson.*

To help explain to the public how cruel the slave trade was and why so many people died during the 'Middle Passage' the abolitionist Thomas Clarkson asked a carpenter to build him two models of a British slave ship called the *Brooks*. This ship had been officially measured by the Royal Navy. It was three times the size of the *Zong* and was typical of the sort of ships being used by British slave traders at that time. The upper decks of the models could be removed to reveal the slave decks below, upon which had been painted an image of the captives, 482 men, women and children shackled tightly together and attached to the deck. This was how many Africans the *Brooks* had actually carried on one of its slave-trading journeys. But in 1783 the *Brooks* had set sail with 609 enslaved Africans on board, 158 more than she had been built to accommodate.

Clarkson took one of his model ships with him when he travelled around the country speaking at abolitionist meetings. He gave the other to William Wilberforce, who used it to educate his fellow MPs in Parliament on the realities of the slave trade. You can still see William Wilberforce's model of the *Brooks*. It is on display at the Wilberforce House Museum in his home town of Hull. An image of the slave ship *Brooks* was also produced by the abolitionists and made into a poster. This became one of the most famous images in the battle against slavery. It was printed and reprinted thousands of time and in the centuries since the slave trade it has been the inspiration

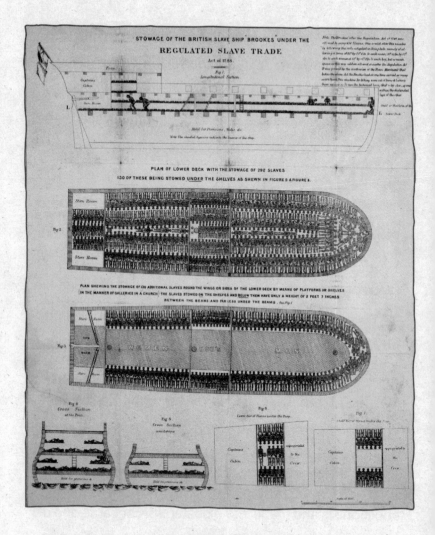

This famous poster of the Brooks was distributed across the world as part of the abolitionist campaign.

for many artists. It even appeared on the cover of an album by Bob Marley.

One effect of the *Zong* massacre was that it increased pressure to introduce controls on the slave traders. In 1788 the government passed the Slave Trade Act. It was the first small victory of the abolitionist movement. The law set limits for the number of slaves that could be carried on a slave ship and forced every slave ship to have a doctor on board who had to keep a log of all sickness and any deaths that took place among the enslaved people.

The Rights of Man

The last years of the eighteenth century were years of revolution, starting in France in 1789. The revolutionaries demanded freedom, equality and the 'rights of man'. These same ideas reached France's slave colonies in the West Indies. In 1791 the half a million people who were enslaved on the island of St Domingue – modern Haiti – rose up to seize their freedom. Their revolution lasted until 1804 and was the largest slave rebellion in history. The cane fields of St Domingue produced around 30 per cent of all the world's sugar. In the first weeks of the uprising over a thousand of the plantations upon which Black people had been forced to work were destroyed. Led by their general, Toussaint Louverture, the former slaves were victorious and the French slave colony of St Domingue became the free black republic of Haiti. Slave owners across the West Indies and America were shocked that a slave rebellion had been successful. There were also slave rebellions in Britain's colonies in the West Indies. The enslaved people in Jamaica, St Vincent, Demerara (now Guyana), Grenada and St Lucia all rebelled. The enslaved were determined to resist their oppression and weakened the slave system whenever they got the chance. The slave owners were determined to fight to defend slavery.

The abolitionists remained focused on ending the slave trade. William Wilberforce led the struggle to pass the law that would end the trade. He made his first attempted to

William Wilberforce, abolitionist and MP, aged twenty-nine.

get Parliament to pass a law to end the trade in 1791. It was easily defeated by 163 votes to 88, partly because a number of MPs were slave owners and others were supporters of the slave traders. Wilberforce tried again the following year but that attempt was also rejected by MPs. Wilberforce kept trying. He introduced bills for the abolition of the slave trade every year between 1794 and 1799. He lost the vote every time. In 1805 yet another bill was defeated in Parliament but by then the political mood had begun to change. Many of the pro-slavery members of Parliament had retired and a new generation had taken their place on the benches of the House of Commons. In 1807 Wilberforce, with the encouragement of the Prime Minister, Lord Grenville, introduced another abolition bill. This time it passed and became law in 1808. The British slave trade that had begun in the 1660s under King Charles II was over.

Gradualism

The abolition of the slave trade was an important victory, but slavery itself remained legal and hundreds of thousands of Black people remained enslaved on the islands of the West Indies. Yet the abolitionists did not start to campaign to have them made free. William

Wilberforce, Thomas Clarkson and almost all of the abolitionists believed in what they called 'gradualism' – which meant that slavery had to be ended gradually, over many years. They suggested that the enslaved people had to be prepared for freedom by being educated and by becoming Christians. Many of the abolitionists now spent their time supporting the work of missionaries who were sent to the West Indies to educate the enslaved and convert them to Christianity.

> They suggested that the enslaved people had to be prepared for freedom by being educated and by becoming Christians

The abolitionists had always believed that if the slave trade was ended the slave owners would treat the enslaved better. That theory was not put to the test. Both the abolitionists and the government set about gathering statistics about West Indian slavery. An act, passed in 1819, required all slaves to be registered. This made it possible to create a census, a list of all the enslaved people. This could be used to see if they were being better treated as it showed how many people died and how many babies were born and if those babies survived their first years.

What the slave census and the investigations by the abolitionists revealed was that after the end of the slave trade the slave owners did not reform slavery. They did not come to see the enslaved people as valuable assets that had to be looked after better. Instead enslaved women and children were compelled to work harder, often doing jobs that demanded greater physical exertion. More women were forced to work in the fields and both women and men who had once worked as servants in the homes of the slave owners were marched to the fields and made to plant, tend and cut sugar cane. Enslaved people were also rented out by one slave owner to another, which meant their families were broken up and they had less time to grow food on their own little patches of land. The end of the slave trade had not made life better for the enslaved people of the British colonies of the West Indies.

Enslaved women and children were compelled to work harder

In 1823 a new generation of abolitionists began their struggle to end slavery itself. Many of the new abolitionists wanted slavery to be ended immediately, not gradually, and many of their leaders were women. One of the most important was Elizabeth Heyrick, a Quaker schoolteacher from Leicester who in 1824 wrote a pamphlet entitled *Immediate, not Gradual Abolition*. Other female abolitionists began a new sugar boycott and organized new waves of abolitionist meetings and petitions.

Rebellion in Jamaica

At Christmas in 1831 events in the West Indies gave the issue of slavery a new and deadly urgency. A rebellion broke out in the west of Jamaica. It was led by Sam Sharpe, an enslaved man who could read and write. He was also a member of a Baptist church. What Sharpe planned was a strike. His modest demand was that the slave owners should pay the enslaved for

> His modest demand was that the slave owners should pay the enslaved for their labour

their labour. They promised one another that they would refuse to work after Christmas 1831 unless the slave owners promised to pay them wages. It was what we today would call non-violent action or civil disobedience. The slave owners had been expecting some form of resistance from the enslaved and they attacked the striking slaves who then rose up. At least 20,000 slaves began to fight for their freedom. Some reports suggested that the final figure was 50,000 or even 60,000. The sugar cane fields were set ablaze and the great houses of the slave owners burnt down. The rebellion lasted two weeks and it took the local garrison of the British Army three months to completely end the fighting.

At least 20,000 slaves began to fight for their freedom

More than 300 rebels were killed and at least 340 more, including Sam Sharpe, were executed. A further 140 were shipped off as convicts to New South Wales in Australia. Over a million pounds' worth of damage had been done

'Am I not a man and a brother?' became a famous slogan
of the abolitionist movement

and the slave owners blamed the Baptist missionaries who had spread Christianity among the enslaved. After the rebellion it was clear that if the enslaved were not emancipated there would be a second and even greater rebellion in Jamaica.

By the summer of 1833 the slave owners knew that slavery was coming to an end. For years they had demanded that if the enslaved were to be freed the slave owners would have to be paid compensation for the loss of the human property. The government finally agreed to that demand and promised to give twenty million pounds to the 46,000 slave owners. The former slaves received nothing.

> The government promised to give twenty million pounds to the 46,000 slave owners. The former slaves received nothing

While the government began the huge task of distributing the compensation money the enslaved people remained where they were, working on the plantations. Under the law passed to end slavery they were not to be freed straight away. Instead a new system called apprenticeship was invented. This meant that the former slaves had to continue working for the same masters for another six years and without being paid. Eventually the government agreed to end the apprenticeship system early and on 1 August 1838, 800,000 enslaved people were finally freed. In parts of the West Indies today 1 August is celebrated as Emancipation Day.

VICTORIANS

1837–1901

By the time Queen Victoria came to the throne in 1837, Britain had already made laws to ban both the slave trade and slavery itself. The next year, enslaved people in the British Empire would finally be free.

The West Africa Squadron

It took more than laws to stop the slave trade. In 1808, when the ban on the trade started, the Royal Navy stepped up to enforce it. Suddenly, the Navy switched from protecting British slave ships to hunting them down. Any British slave ship caught by the Navy's new West Africa Squadron could have its sailors arrested and the

HMS Pluto patrolled the coast of Africa intercepting slave ships as part of the West Africa Squadron.

captives freed. Britain had been the world's biggest slave-trading country; now it had an anti-slave trade police force.

Soon Britain began to make agreements with other countries' governments to ban their own slave trades, and the West Africa Squadron went after ships from those countries too. It wasn't an easy fight. Countries like Portugal, Brazil and Spain all shipped more enslaved people to make up for the end of the British trade. There was far too much money to be made from the slave trade for people to give it up entirely. While most British ships and companies did stop trading in enslaved people, British merchants still invested their money in slave-powered businesses, and British companies still made chains for use on enslaved people.

British merchants still invested their money in slave-powered businesses, and British companies still made chains for use on enslaved people

One problem was that the slave traders could afford much faster ships than the Navy patrols, and often escaped from them. The West Africa Squadron's best ships often started out being used by slave traders. When they captured a fast clipper called the *Black Joke*, the Navy turned it from a slave ship into a slave-catching ship. In 1829, the *Black Joke* chased a bigger and better-armed Spanish slave ship for thirty-one hours, day and night, and then freed the 466 people held on board. The daring chase made headlines back home in Britain, and the *Black Joke* became the West Africa Squadron's most famous ship. Some of the crew on board were Africans from the Kru people of Liberia, who used to make their living as fishermen and were skilled sailors. Later in the nineteenth century there would be communities of Kru sailors in ports like Liverpool and London.

The West Africa Squadron operated for nearly sixty years. The Squadron only stopped a small proportion of the ships crossing the Atlantic, but it made a huge difference to the roughly 160,000 people it freed. Many of these people made their home in the city of Freetown, Sierra Leone, where the West Africa Squadron had its base. They were called 'recaptives' because they had been captured twice: once by slave traders, and again by the Royal Navy. Freetown became full of freed Africans from different countries and tribes, with many languages and cultures. There was also a strong Christian culture in Freetown, where the British charity the Church Missionary Society taught the Bible and set up schools. The Society even renamed recaptive children after people who gave money to them. Freetown was shaped by Britain and by the many thousands of people whose lives had been turned upside down by the slave trade and the fight against it.

— III —

Sarah Forbes Bonetta

While the West Africa Squadron was chasing slave traders, the British government was trying to replace the slave trade with other kinds of legal trade with Africa, in goods like palm oil, cotton or ivory. The city of Lagos in modern Nigeria became the main trading port of West Africa, and the Christian Saro community which came to Lagos from Sierra Leone was at the centre of these trades. Britain also sent its agents to talk to the local leaders who traded in enslaved people. In 1850, Captain Frederick Forbes of the West Africa Squadron went to the kingdom of Dahomey to meet King Ghezo, to persuade him to give up the slave trade. Ghezo had made Dahomey rich through slavery, and not surprisingly, he said no. Instead he gave Frederick Forbes presents to take back to Queen Victoria, including a young enslaved girl of about seven years old.

On the way to England, the girl was given a new name: Sarah Forbes (after Frederick) Bonetta (after the ship they sailed on). Sarah Forbes Bonetta was introduced to

15 September 1862: Sarah Forbes Bonetta with her husband James Davies.

Queen Victoria, who liked her instantly and wrote in her diary that Sarah was 'sharp & intelligent'. The Queen paid for her to be educated in Freetown, Sierra Leone. Sarah Forbes Bonetta soon came back to England, and lived in Brighton. In 1862 she met and married James Pinson Labulo Davies, a successful Black businessman who grew up in Sierra Leone and made his fortune in Lagos. James and Sarah's wedding was reported in the newspapers, and their picture was taken by a celebrity photographer. They had a daughter, named Victoria, whose godmother was Queen Victoria herself. When Sarah died, the Queen paid for her daughter to go to private school in England. Sarah and James Davies were both undoubtedly African, and they were also British, mixing at the highest levels of British life.

The World Anti-Slavery Convention

The campaigners who had fought for the end of the slave trade, and then for the abolition of slavery itself, were not satisfied with the end of slavery in Britain's colonies. The job was still unfinished. In 1840, three years after Queen

Thomas Clarkson speaking at the World Anti-Slavery Convention in 1840.

Victoria was crowned, the World Anti-Slavery Convention was held in London. Men from around the world spoke about the evils of slavery (women speakers were not allowed). One speaker, Henry Beckford, had been enslaved himself until just a few years before the convention. He said, 'I was a slave for twenty-eight years, but look at me and work on. There are other parts of the world where slavery now exists, but I trust the negroes there will soon become freemen as I am today.' The Anti-Slavery Convention agreed that Britain had done a wonderful thing by abolishing slavery. They also agreed that the next task was to end slavery all around the world.

The most obvious place to start this campaign with was America. The USA had been independent from Britain for over sixty years, but the two countries were still very closely linked. Black people in the USA were already celebrating Britain's ban on slavery. While white Americans threw a party for their Independence Day each year on 4 July, free Black Americans celebrated 1 August: the day the slaves had been freed in the British Empire in 1838. Enslaved people in America saw Britain's colonies in the West Indies as places of hope. In 1841, a group of 128 slaves on an American ship called the *Creole* rose up against the crew. They managed to take control of the ship and sail it to the British-owned Bahamas where they would be free. The British anti-slavery movement wanted this freedom

> Free Black Americans celebrated 1 August: the day the slaves had been freed in the British Empire in 1838

for everyone in the USA. They began a campaign that would bring people from both sides of the Atlantic together to work towards that goal.

Henry 'Box' Brown

In the 1840s and 1850s, African-American speakers toured Britain to get support for this campaign, and many published best-selling books. Most of them had been enslaved themselves, and could give first-hand details of what it was like. Henry 'Box' Brown was one of these star speakers who also wrote his life story. Brown got his nickname from the dramatic way he freed himself from slavery: he sent himself by mail in a wooden box from Richmond in Virginia to the northern city of Philadelphia, where slavery was illegal. The box was less than a metre long, and Brown spent twenty-seven hours folded inside it. Henry Brown came to Britain in 1850, published a book about his life, and spoke about it in theatres all around the country. He even took his box with him and appeared from inside it on stage. Brown's story also shows how dangerous it was to be Black in America, even in the

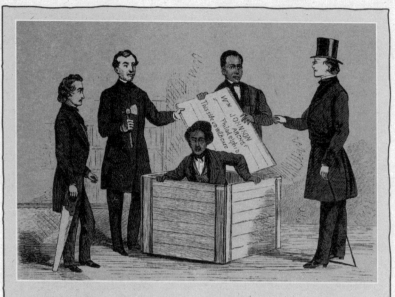

Henry 'Box' Brown emerges from the box he used to mail himself to freedom.

northern states which had banned slavery. He came to Britain after a law was passed in the USA called the Fugitive Slave Act. The law made it illegal for anyone to stop slaveholders hunting down escaped slaves, even if they had gone to places where they were free. For people who had been enslaved, like Henry Brown, this meant that their old 'owners' could have hired men to catch them and take them back into slavery. It was a good reason to head for safety in Britain.

Frederick Douglass

The most famous African-American speaker to tour Britain in the 1840s was Frederick Douglass. Douglass escaped from slavery in 1838 and became a preacher

A young Frederick Douglass in 1848.

and anti-slavery campaigner. He wrote a book about his life and then came to Britain to speak all around the country, and to raise money for his newspaper *The North Star*. He also came to get further away from the man who still legally owned him. Douglass became a star, and his powerful speeches gave the anti-slavery campaign in Britain a huge boost. The friends he made in Britain changed his life as well. Ellen and Anna Richardson were Quakers from Newcastle, who raised £150 to buy Frederick Douglass from his former 'owner'. Some people thought this was wrong, and said Douglass and the Richardsons were acting as if it was all right to buy and sell people in the first place. But Frederick Douglass was now legally free in America, and safe to go back home.

Like other African Americans, Douglass said it was a relief to be treated so equally in Britain. The writer Harriet Jacobs wrote that in Britain 'for the first time in my life I was in a place where I was treated according to my deportment, without reference to my complexion'. The anti-slavery movement was popular in Britain in the

1840s and 1850s, but that didn't mean that British people were never racist – it was possible to be against slavery and still think white people were better than Black people. Charles Dickens, the superstar Victorian novelist whose books had a strong sense of right and wrong, visited America and thought slavery was horrific. But he also wrote about Black people in racist ways.

Uncle Tom's Cabin

Victorians loved American books and music, and through them they learned about the horrors of slavery in the USA. They also learned some racist ideas about Black people. The best-selling book in Victorian Britain, other than the Bible, was *Uncle Tom's Cabin* by the white American author Harriet Beecher Stowe. It told the story of enslaved Black people escaping slavery, and of Uncle Tom, who is murdered by his owner but still forgives him. The characters in *Uncle Tom's Cabin* can seem like stereotypes to modern readers, but at the time the book made its millions of readers feel the emotions of a family being split apart by slavery. When Harriet Beecher Stowe visited Britain in

An edition of Uncle Tom's Cabin *from around 1908.*

1853, she was given a petition against slavery, from the women of Britain to the women of the USA.

African-American music was hugely popular in Victorian Britain. There was a craze for banjo playing, and the Prince of Wales is believed to have had lessons from the African-American banjo stars the Bohee Brothers. A choir of Black students from Tennessee called the Fisk Jubilee Singers toured Britain in the 1870s and 1880s, singing in front of packed audiences. The 'spiritual' songs they introduced to Britain, including *Nobody Knows the Trouble I See* and *Swing Low, Sweet Chariot*, became a much-loved part of musical culture in this country.

Even before the Fisk Jubilee Singers brought their genuine African-American music to British listeners, white performers were painting their faces black to copy the music and dancing of enslaved Americans. They were called 'minstrels', and they used stereotypes about childlike Black people to make their white audiences laugh. Sometimes, the minstrels spoke out against slavery – but the racism of their exaggerated 'blackface', movements and voices also stuck with their British fans. Minstrels stayed popular in Britain for a shockingly long time: *The Black and White Minstrel Show* ran on British TV until the 1970s.

When Frederick Douglass came back to Britain at the end of the 1850s, he said that it was a more racist country than it had been fifteen years before. He blamed the minstrel acts, among other people. But there were also new kinds of racism appearing, that claimed to have a basis in science.

A writer named Thomas Carlyle set out his version of the 'new racism' in the 1840s and 1850s. He wrote about the sugar islands of the West Indies, where the plantations were making less money than ever before. In reality there were lots of reasons for this, including the world economy and tax changes. Instead, Carlyle blamed the Black workers who had left the plantations after the end of slavery to start their own small farms. He said that Black people were lazy and inferior to white people, and were made by God to serve them. He even thought that abolishing slavery had been a mistake after all.

Carlyle said that Black people were lazy and inferior to white people, and were made by God to serve them

Around this time, scientists were developing new theories which would be used to say that racism like Carlyle's was based on science. Charles Darwin published his famous work on evolution, *On The Origin of Species*, in 1859. The 'Social Darwinists' twisted his ideas to say that Black people must have evolved to be inferior to white people. If Africans had evolved to live in hot parts of the world, some thought, it also made sense that they were the best people to work on plantations in the West Indies. Darwin himself disagreed with these ideas, and was against slavery all his life – but Social Darwinism had brought poisonous new arguments to British racism.

The new racism took shape in some respectable-sounding organizations. In 1863, a group called the Anthropological Society of London was formed. Some of the Society's members believed that the different 'races' of humans were basically different species. They argued against ending slavery, and said that while Africans could be clever when they were children, their brains were limited and Black adults could never be as intelligent as white people. They explained

> Some of the Society's members believed that the different 'races' of humans were basically different species

away brilliant Black individuals, saying that they were exceptions or that they must have had white ancestors.

People in Jamaica were about to take a stand which pushed these arguments into the spotlight. More than twenty years after the end of slavery, life for Black people on the island was extremely hard. Black Jamaicans had no votes or power and it was difficult for them to own land. A group of Black Jamaicans asked the Queen for permission to grow food, cotton and tobacco on government-owned land, and then sell it to England, but the government would not allow it. They suggested that the Jamaicans were lazy for not wanting to work for white landowners on plantations.

In 1865, there was a riot in the small town of Morant Bay in a poor part of Jamaica. When a local man was taken to court for farming on land that the owner had abandoned, there was an angry protest at the courthouse. The authorities then tried to arrest a local preacher called Paul Bogle and several people died in the riot that followed.

Fields of cotton and tobacco.

In itself, the Morant Bay Uprising was not a large rebellion. But the white rulers of Jamaica were constantly worried that the Black majority would rise up against them. The governor of Jamaica, Edward Eyre, thought that Morant Bay was part of a rebellious plot by Black people all over the island. He took violent revenge on the people of Jamaica, with six weeks of arrests, unfair trials and executions.

Once the news of Eyre's brutal overreaction came out in Britain, people took sides. Some, including Charles Darwin, called for him to be put on trial. Thomas Carlyle, along with writers such as Charles Dickens, defended Governor Eyre. For the 'new racists' in the Anthropological Society of London, the Morant Bay Uprising was proof that Black people were inferior and needed to be controlled, with violence if necessary.

The Industrial Revolution

In spite of the rise of the 'new racism', many people in Victorian Britain still felt proud of their country's fight against slavery. In the 1860s, the country was forced to face up to the fact that Britain's economy still relied on slavery.

In the middle of the nineteenth century, the UK was a powerhouse of industry. Britain's Industrial Revolution had begun in the Midlands and north of England around a hundred years before, and centred around using machines to turn cotton into thread and cloth. It is often forgotten that these industries were partly powered by slavery from the beginning. Mills and factories had been built using money made by investing in the slave trade.

There were around 4,500 mills in Lancashire processing cotton.

> Although Britain was proud of its history in abolishing slavery, British businesses still relied on cotton grown by enslaved people

Most of the cotton was grown by enslaved workers. Even after British slavery ended in 1838, British industry was still part of this system. Although Britain was proud of its history in abolishing slavery, British businesses still relied on cotton grown by enslaved people.

By the 1860s, cotton was the UK's main export. Manchester had earned the nickname 'Cottonopolis', and more than 400,000 people worked in the cotton industry around the city. Most of the cotton they worked with had been picked by enslaved people in the southern states of the USA, where the climate was right for the cotton plant. The cotton plantations in America and the cotton mills and factories in Britain were two halves of the same industry. The Black enslaved workers who picked the cotton may never have come to Britain, but they were as much a part of British history as Black Georgians or Victorians.

All this meant that when the American Civil War began, it shook the north of England as well. In 1861 the northern and southern states of the USA went to war with each other. A large part of the split between them was that the northern states had abolished slavery, and made money from industry instead, while the southern states used enslaved people on the plantations which brought them their wealth. From the start of the war, the northern states began a blockade, stopping ships from using the southern ports. This meant that cotton could no longer be sent from America to Britain. By the end of 1862 the British factories' stores of cotton were running out, more than half of the looms for weaving cloth in Lancashire were not being used because of the shortage, and hundreds of thousands of people in northern England were out of work. This was known as the 'Cotton Famine'. Soup kitchens opened to feed the hungry and charities supported workers who had no money coming in.

The British government decided not to take sides in the American Civil War, but British people often did. Many people who worked in the cotton industry supported the South because the North's blockade was causing so many problems. The British port of Liverpool had grown rich from the slave trade and was the place where American slave-produced cotton was unloaded from ships. Merchants there were strong supporters of the South. They found ways around the blockade, built ships for the South, and sent them guns.

> **Liverpool had grown rich from the slave trade and was the place where American slave-produced cotton was unloaded. Merchants there were strong supporters of the South**

Even though the blockade was stopping the cotton that Britain's mills needed, some mill workers and mill owners backed the North anyway. In the Lancashire town of Rochdale, where there was a tradition of campaigning against slavery, the people were especially loud about their support for the North. After the President of the USA, Abraham Lincoln, announced that the slaves would be freed if the North won the Civil War, a group of workers from Manchester held a meeting. They wrote to the President to say that they supported him, and that the war and their own poverty would be worth it if it brought freedom for Black Americans. The North did indeed win the war, and banned slavery across the USA in January 1865.

The Scramble for Africa

In the 1880s, the British fight against slavery around the world became part of a new phase of the empire. For decades, Britain had been working to replace the slave trade with other kinds of trade with Africa. Now the British would take this project much further. They would take control over much more of the continent than ever before.

The leaders of Europe, the USA and the Ottoman Empire met in 1884 to make a plan to colonize Africa. This was the Berlin Conference, a meeting which was the beginning of the 'Scramble for Africa': the years in which European empires took control over the continent. No African leaders were invited to the conference.

Deciding Africa's future at the Berlin Conference of 1884–1885.

For the European countries, new colonies in Africa would bring new markets to sell things to; money and power to compete with other empires; and land for Europeans to settle on. Britain also said that controlling parts of Africa would be part of the British mission to end slavery there. The Prince of Wales, speaking at an anti-slavery meeting in London, said that 'the best chance of a complete abolition of slavery will lie in civilization, in opening up those great countries, Asia and Africa, many parts of which are now known to but few Europeans'. The idea which the Prince didn't need to explain was that white people knew best what 'civilization' should be. To bring 'civilization', Christianity and trade to African people, Britain would take control of their land.

Up until this point, much of Africa had not been explored by Europeans. The lands away from the coast were still unknown and mysterious. But by the 1880s, the Victorian age of scientific progress was in full swing. Exploring and colonizing Africa seemed like a tempting challenge on the way to a more modern world.

New science and technology powered Europeans' takeover of Africa. Steam riverboats took their armies straight to the heart of the continent. New medicines helped Europeans survive tropical diseases like malaria. Advanced machine guns and improved rifles let European soldiers win battles against much bigger armies of Africans.

New science and technology powered Europeans' takeover of Africa

The Scramble for Africa happened quickly. In 1870, only 10 per cent of African land was controlled by Europeans. By 1900, only 10 per cent of African land was ruled by Africans, and the rest belonged to Europe. Britain had been especially successful: 45 million people, or one-third of all Africans, became British colonial subjects. That meant that there were more British subjects in Africa than in the United Kingdom.

People back home in Britain followed the dramatic growth of the British Empire. The stories of British explorers, hunters, and soldiers in Africa were told as heroic adventures in an exotic land. Newspaper reporters turned colonization into entertainment, and the public loved it. Maps showed the land ruled by the British Empire, all around the world, coloured in pink (it should have been red like British Army uniforms, but the mapmakers lightened the colour so that place names would stand out better). It was exciting for people in Britain to feel that their country could rule so much of the world, and for some people it proved that the British were special.

The people of Britain were fascinated by the new things they were learning about the people of Africa. Each new tribe the British met as they explored was studied and put into categories. Scientists discovered that different 'races' had different sizes and shapes of skull, and used this knowledge to come up with theories about racial 'types'. Each 'type' was said to have its own characteristics. The Ndebele people were thought to be savage warriors, the Yoruba were supposed to be obsessed with money, and the Zulu were believed to be superstitious. Racial theories like this mixed with the ideas of the Social Darwinists. Increasingly, people believed that if the British were ruling over so much of the world, it must be because they had evolved to be stronger and more intelligent than other races.

Some people from parts of Africa which Europeans had recently conquered came to Britain as a kind of museum exhibit. Big exhibitions were popular in the late nineteenth and early twentieth centuries. Millions of visitors bought tickets to see exotic objects, animals and people from

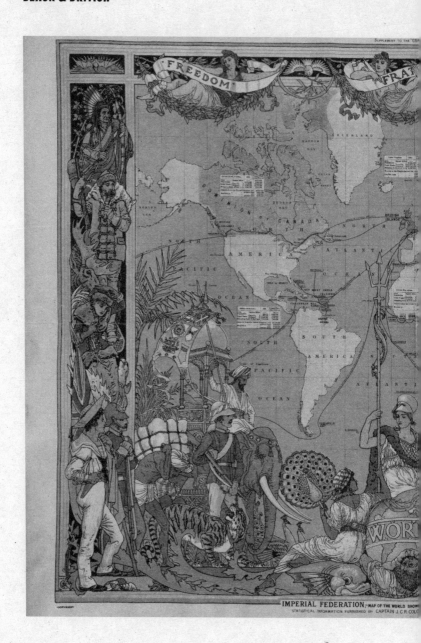

Senegalese wrestlers perform for visitors in a mock-African village built for a colonial exhibition in Paris.

around the world. Colonial exhibitions often included 'native villages', sometimes now called human zoos. These were recreated village scenes with huts, in which real Africans acted out their daily lives back in Africa. The villages were often less real than they seemed. In 1904, a group of around a hundred Somalis lived in a village in the Bradford Exhibition for several months. When they left, the local newspaper reported that a surprising number of the Somalis actually spoke English and wore European suits. They were professional performers, and the leaders of the group were making good money. After Bradford, they were on their way to an exhibition in Belgium. They were not the only group of African performers to travel around European exhibitions as their job.

Royal visitors

African kings and chiefs also visited Britain in the later part of Queen Victoria's reign. The media and the public found these Black royals fascinating. One visit in particular made stars out of the royal visitors. In 1895, a group of three kings from southern Africa made an extraordinary journey to Britain. They came to stand up to the British colonialist who wanted to take their lands.

The man the kings were worried about was Cecil Rhodes, Prime Minister of the Cape Colony in today's South Africa and a driving force in the Scramble for Africa. Rhodes believed the British were superior to other people and that the world would be better if Britain ruled more of it. He made a fortune in diamond mining, used a private army to take land for his British South Africa Company, and dreamed of making Africa British all the way from the southern tip of Africa to Egypt in the north, with a railway to connect them. He even had a country – Rhodesia (now Zimbabwe) – named after him along the way. By 1895, Rhodes had his eyes on Bechuanaland, now known as Botswana, which was already officially a 'protectorate' of the British government. Rhodes wanted his own private company to take over Bechuanaland instead and sell land to white settlers.

Rhodes wanted his own private company to take over Bechuanaland instead and sell land to white settlers

The rulers of Bechuanaland knew this would be a disaster for them, so King Khama III of the BagammaNgwato people came up with a plan to stop Rhodes. Together with two other Bechuanaland kings, Sebele I of the Kwêna people and Bathoen I of the Bangwaketse, King Khama went to Britain. His aim was to persuade the government to protect Bechuanaland from Cecil Rhodes. Khama wrote to the Colonial Secretary that '[Rhodes's] Company does

From left to right: Sebele I of the Kwêna people, Bathoen I of the Bangwaketse, Khama III of the BagammaNgwato and the Reverend William Charles Willoughby of the London Missionary Society.

not love Black people . . . it loves only to take the country of the Black people and sell it to others that it may see gain'. The three kings spent weeks travelling around the country, giving talks, going to dinners, meeting businessmen and politicians, talking to the press, and raising awareness of their cause. It helped that King Khama was Christian, educated, and didn't drink alcohol – all of which impressed respectable Victorians. Positive press reports helped turn the kings into celebrities. They were able to make a deal with the British government: they would allow the railway to be built on their land, they would be paid properly for it, and most importantly Bechuanaland would stay 'under the protection of the Queen' and not be ruled by Cecil Rhodes. King Khama had managed to talk to the British people who might disagree with Rhodes, and he had taken on the British Empire on his own terms.

There were Black Victorians in ordinary life, as well as celebrities. Most Black people in Victorian Britain lived in London or one of a few port cities, and came from either the West Indies, the USA or Sierra Leone. Some were born in Britain, others came to study, or as sailors. By the end of the century, universities in Durham, London, Cambridge and Liverpool were teaching African students, often in medicine and law. Black doctors, like John Alcindor from Trinidad, began working in British hospitals.

Some Black Victorians found their way into British life by serving in the army and navy. In 1885, British soldiers from the Durham Light Infantry fighting in Sudan found an abandoned boy and looked after him. They took him back to England with them and gave him a new name, Jimmy Durham, after his regiment. Jimmy stayed with the army and served in India. When he came back to Britain, he settled down and started a family in the north-east of England.

Other Black Victorians worked as musicians and performers, like the African Americans who brought their styles of music and culture to Britain. One of the most successful Victorian Black entertainers was neither

Pablo Fanque, the Black circus performer and entrepreneur depicted in the Illustrated London News, *20 March 1847.*

American nor a musician, but a circus star from Norwich with an African father. William Darby joined the circus at an early age and started using an exotic stage name. As Pablo Fanque he became an expert horse rider and trapeze artist, and soon ran his own circus. He became famous again in the twentieth century when he was mentioned in the Beatles song 'Being for the Benefit of Mr Kite', which was inspired by a circus poster for one of Pablo Fanque's shows in 1843.

The Black population in Victorian Britain was small in numbers. But the number of Black British subjects in Africa and the West Indies was vast and growing. In the next century, many more of them would travel to the small country at the heart of the empire.

THE FIRST WORLD WAR

1914-1918

The picture most British people have of the First World War is of soldiers fighting in muddy trenches in northern Europe. But as its name suggests, the war took place around the world. It was fought in the Middle East, Asia and Africa, as well as at sea. What began as a local quarrel in south-east Europe in the summer of 1914 quickly spread and became a clash between empires. Soldiers from all over the world fought and died, including men from the British colonies in Africa and the West Indies.

Britain and Germany both had colonies in Africa which joined the war along with their European governments. The first soldier in the British Army to fire a shot in the land war was Lance Corporal Alhaji Grunshi from the Gold Coast (today's Ghana). He was taking part in an attack on the German colony of Togoland in East Africa. The last soldiers from the German army to surrender at the end of the war in November 1918 were also in Africa.

The war in Africa covered a massive area of land. The army had to travel many miles with all their weapons and kit, so they recruited one million Africans to work as carriers. Men from the West Indies could join the British West Indies Regiment, which was created in 1915. They fought in Africa and also in the Middle East, but when the regiment's soldiers were sent to France it was as a labour corps. They were put to work digging trenches, building roads, and moving supplies. This was important and dangerous work, but it was not what they had trained for, and it revealed a lot about the way the empire worked.

The British Army had a problem for most of the war: they badly needed more men to fight in Western Europe. Over a million men volunteered at the start of the war, but so many were killed that there was a constant need for new recruits. Britain introduced a system of conscription in 1916, to force men to join the army. Conscription was not used in the British colonies in Africa and the West Indies. In both those areas, people were more enthusiastic about the war than the government had expected.

West Indian men were especially keen to fight for Britain in the war. There was a feeling of wanting to help Britain, the 'mother country'. Many people felt loyal to the British royal family and saw the British Empire as an empire of freedom. One Jamaican who wrote to the *Jamaica Times* newspaper in 1914 argued that 'for the love that we hold for the British flag . . . we should fight as brave men and die as heroes'. At the same

West Indian men were especially keen to fight for Britain in the war

Men of the British West Indies Regiment in camp on the Albert-Amiens Road, September 1916.

time, the West Indies were still poor and there was not much work available. The army offered steady wages as well as adventure. All these reasons drove some men from the West Indies to buy tickets for ships to Britain, or even stow away illegally on board, so that they could try to join the army when they arrived.

For some people, it seemed obvious that Britain should welcome these volunteers, and put them into new regiments to fight in Europe where they were needed. The need for new recruits became increasingly urgent as the war went on. There were sixty thousand British casualties on the first day of the Battle of the Somme in 1916. Despite the need, the British government was not at all pleased that so many West Indians and Africans wanted to join the army.

> It seemed obvious that Britain should welcome these volunteers, and put them into new regiments to fight in Europe

They had one major reason for not letting Black regiments fight in Europe: it would break a basic rule of colonialism. Giving weapons and training to Black men from the colonies, and sending them to fight Europeans, went against the colonial rule that Black people should not be permitted to kill white people. What the British feared was that Black soldiers who were trained to fight would expect better treatment within the British Empire after the war. The British also feared losing the support of white South Africans who were fighting against the Germans in Africa and in Europe. As a result of this, the British Army did not create Black regiments to fight in Europe.

In spite of this, on some occasions Black servicemen did join regiments alongside white men and fight with them in Europe. Both Black British men and others from colonies outside Britain managed to join up if the officers in charge chose to let them. Ernest Marke from Sierra Leone managed to join the army in 1918 even though he was African. It didn't even seem to matter that at only fifteen, he was officially too young to fight.

Two brothers from Jamaica, Norman and Roy Manley, were students in Britain when they joined up to serve in the Royal Field Artillery. They both fought in France, where Roy was killed, but Norman survived. He later became a politician, serving as the Chief Minister and then Premier of Jamaica.

Walter Tull

The most famous Black British soldier of the First World War was Walter Tull. Born in Kent, his father was from Barbados where his grandfather had been enslaved. Twenty-six-year-old Tull was already a famous footballer when he joined the army in 1914. He was quickly promoted, and went to France to fight with his regiment. In 1916, he was treated for a mental condition which we would now call post-traumatic stress disorder. He even became an officer, even though the Army rules said that all officers should be 'of pure European descent' – meaning white. The rules could be bent for the right person, and Walter Tull was officer material. He led his men as a second lieutenant until March 1918, when he was killed in action in France.

Post-war ingratitude

After the war, the African and West Indian regiments which had fought for Britain were not invited to march in the official Victory Parade in London. Many Black soldiers went home disappointed by the way they had been

Walter Tull

The Victory Parade in London, 19 July 1919. Black soldiers were not allowed to take part.

treated during and after the war. They had volunteered to serve Britain when they were needed. They had met, worked, and fought with people from across the empire. But they had also been reminded that they were seen as less important than white people. They had been treated unfairly, given different duties and sometimes paid less, and after the war their contribution was ignored. These experiences gave many West Indians and Africans a new view of the British Empire.

Some white British people were also unhappy about how Black people from Africa and the West Indies had been treated in the war, but for different reasons. For them, the fact that Black troops had fought in the war was a threat. They wanted Africans and West Indians to go back to their proper place. The war had also brought more Black people to the cities of Europe. There had been only a few thousand Black people living in Britain at the start of the war, mostly in London and a few port cities. After the war ended in 1918, there were around 20,000 Black people around the country. Some were sailors who had served on the ships that had brought the food and weapons which Britain needed in wartime. Others had come to work in the factories. But now that the war was over, times were hard and British soldiers came home to find that there were not enough jobs or houses for them. It was easy to blame this on immigrants, and especially on the Black immigrants.

> After the war ended in 1918, there were around 20,000 Black people in Britain

These feelings soon led to violence. In 1919, just over two months after the war had ended, Black and white sailors were waiting together in Glasgow to be given work. The white sailors shouted insults to the Black sailors, who they thought were taking jobs that should be theirs. When a fight started, local people joined in against the Black sailors. Violence soon broke out in other port cities too, with large groups of white people attacking Black sailors and their families. The riots spread to Liverpool, where several hundred Black men were out of work. On one night of fighting, someone called the police. They raided a house, and a young Black man snuck out of a back door to escape. He was a twenty-four-year-old sailor from Bermuda named Charles Wootton. The angry crowd out in the street spotted him running away, and chased him for over a mile to the dock. At the water's edge, he either fell or was pushed into the water. Before a policeman could reach him, Charles Wootton was hit on the head by a stone thrown from the crowd and died. No one was ever arrested for his murder.

As the riots and attacks went on, violent crowds attacked more Black people and raided their homes. Hundreds of Black people in Liverpool asked the police to arrest them to keep them safe. The police started to keep lists of all the Black people living in the city to keep track of them, and gave out registration cards which Black sailors had to have to get work. Over the next few years, laws were passed in Britain targeting Black people, and Indian, Chinese and Arab people from around the British Empire, who could all be forced to leave the country if they didn't have the right paperwork. These laws, added to the violent riots and to their treatment during the war, suggested that Black people were in some way foreign. They might be British subjects, and they might even have volunteered to risk their lives for Britain in the war, but it was not clear if Black people would ever be seen as truly British.

> They might be British subjects, and they might even have volunteered to risk their lives for Britain in the war, but it was not clear if Black people would ever be seen as truly British

THE SECOND WORLD WAR

1939–1945

The Second World War changed life in Britain dramatically. One of the many changes was an enormous rise – for a short time – in the country's Black population. At the end of the last war there were around 20,000 Black people living in Britain. By the beginning of June 1944, that number had jumped by more than six times, to 150,000. There was one clear reason for this: the US Army had arrived.

When Hitler's forces conquered France in 1940, Britain and the other Allied powers had to retreat. By 1942, the

130,000 African-American GIs were stationed in Britain during the Second World War.

USA had joined the Allies in the war, and together they planned to fight back against Hitler in Europe. As part of this, the US Army (which included the US Air Force) began to arrive in Britain in May 1942. Around 10 per cent of their soldiers were African American..

In the southern states of the USA, and in the US Army, Black and white people were not allowed to mix. This forced separation by race is known as segregation. When the American troops came to Britain, Black and white soldiers would mostly live in separate camps, eat in separate canteens, and spend their free time in separate army clubs.

> In the US Army Black and white people were not allowed to mix

The government worried that British people would not agree with segregation, and allowing the US Army to bring segregation to Britain would be likely to anger Black British people, West Indians and Africans, including those who came to fight or work for Britain in the war. Once they were invited, though, the Americans were free to bring whichever troops they liked and in their camps the US Army's rules applied.

The US soldiers were known as 'GIs'. (The initials are often believed to stand for 'government issue', though the name may have come from the army cleaning buckets which were stamped 'GI' for 'galvanized iron'.) The GIs had come to help Britain to win the war, and so the British people welcomed them all. The Black GIs often acted differently from the white GIs, who got a reputation for being loud and arrogant, and for complaining about the bad food and poverty they found in Britain. Black GIs were more likely to have experienced poverty back home themselves. Most were also used to being polite to white people for their own safety. Another reason why many British people sided with the Black GIs was because they thought they were treated unfairly, and disagreed with the idea of segregation by race. This seemed especially important when the country was fighting a war for freedom and against the extreme racism of the Nazis.

The arrival of the US Army gave the British government a difficult choice: upset its American allies by speaking out against segregation, or introduce unpopular and obviously racist laws to Britain. In the end, the government decided that it would allow the US Army to segregate its soldiers, but that British authorities would not help enforce those rules. The advice to British service people was to be friendly and polite to the Black GIs, but also to be careful not to cause problems by mixing too closely with them. It was not a good idea, the guidelines said, for white women to go out with Black GIs. And if a British person wanted to invite US soldiers into their home for a friendly visit, they were advised not to invite Black and white GIs at the same time.

> **If a British person wanted to invite US soldiers into their home, they were advised not to invite Black and white GIs at the same time**

The US government also tried to prepare its white soldiers for adjusting to a country without racial segregation. In 1943 they made a film together with the British called *Welcome to Britain*, presented by an actor who played a white soldier showing his fellow GIs around the country. In one scene, an elderly white English woman met a Black American soldier, chatted, shook his hand and asked him to tea. The presenter explained to the audience that though this would be surprising to them, it was normal in Britain. 'That might not happen at home,' he said, 'but the point is we're not at home.'

Many white American GIs still felt that it was up to them to enforce the rules of segregation, even though it wasn't the law in Britain. They would complain to the owners of pubs, restaurants or hotels that were serving Black GIs as guests. One white British woman running a bar had a complaint like this from a white GI. She replied that she would carry on serving Black soldiers, because 'their money is as good as yours, and we prefer their company'.

> Many white American GIs still felt that it was up to them to enforce the rules of segregation

The thing that made white US soldiers most angry was for Black men to get close to white women. While the US Army

A couple dance at Frisco's International Club, Piccadilly, London, c. 1943.

was in Britain ahead of the invasion of Europe, there were many violent assaults on Black GIs who met or dated white British women. While British people believed that in general they were much less racist than Americans, many of them felt that relationships between Black and white people was a step too far. Some British police forces even tried to stop white women from going out with Black US soldiers.

The problems that came with having a segregated army in Britain suddenly came to an end in June 1944. On 6 June, known as D-Day, most of the US Army left for Europe together with British and Canadian forces. They crossed the Channel to land in Normandy to begin the invasion of France. But some of the GIs who had found girlfriends while they were in Britain had left children behind. This meant that there were hundreds of mixed-race children growing up in Britain after the war whose fathers had been Black GIs. After the war, these children and their white British mothers were seen as shameful. They faced discrimination, and many of the children were sent to children's homes.

The African Americans in the US Army were not the only Black people arriving in Britain during the Second World War. Some came to Britain for war work. There was essential work to be done, and not enough people to do it, especially as so many British men of fighting age were serving in the Army, Navy or Air Force. Six hundred foresters came from British Honduras (now Belize) to work in Scotland, 350 electricians and engineers came from the West Indies to work in Liverpool, and more workers followed.

Black men and women from the West Indies and Africa also fought for Britain in the war. The British Army, Royal Navy and Royal Air Force all had rules before the war which tried to keep them only for men of 'pure European descent'. Black campaigners argued against this, and when the war began in September 1939, the government agreed to change the rules during the war. Black men could now serve in the armed forces, including as officers.

More than 12,000 West Indians served in the British forces during the war

More than 12,000 West Indians served in the British forces during the war, including in the Royal Air Force, the Royal Canadian Air Force, the Women's Auxiliary Air Force and the Auxiliary Territorial Service (the women's branch of the British Army). Black servicemen and women who were based in Britain found that, on the whole, they were more likely to get racist abuse from white US soldiers than from white British people.

> Black servicemen and women found that, on the whole, they were more likely to get racist abuse from white US soldiers than from white British people

Sergeant Arthur Walrond came from Barbados, where he had worked as a journalist. He served in Britain during the war as a wireless operator and gunner in the Royal Air Force Volunteer Reserve. One summer night in 1943, Sergeant Walrond went out to a dance. When he asked a white woman to dance with him, he was attacked by two white US soldiers. Sergeant Walrond wrote a powerful letter of complaint to the British government. He wrote: 'I have never been trained to think in terms of nations or races and I had hoped that four years of war would at least have taught the world this lesson.'

Three hundred and seventy-two thousand Africans also served in the British forces. Rather than being sent to fight in Europe, the African regiments mostly fought in colonies in Africa and Asia. The Royal West African Frontier Force, or RWAFF, fought against the Italians in East Africa. Soldiers from East African countries fought in the King's African Rifles, or KAR. The KAR also fought against the Italians in East Africa, and helped to capture Madagascar from the Vichy French who were on the side of the Nazis. Both the RWAFF and the KAR also fought in Burma (now also known as Myanmar) against the Japanese. This was the first time that the African regiments of the British Army had been allowed to fight outside Africa. They were a great success, and several of their soldiers were given medals for their service.

By the end of the Second World War, some British attitudes to Black British subjects had not changed. The government still preferred not to send Black regiments to fight in Europe. Many people still saw relationships between Black and white partners as shameful. But there had been changes too. After so many people from all around the world had fought and died to defeat the extreme racism of Hitler and the Nazis, it was clear how dangerous racist myths could be.

THE TWENTIETH CENTURY

Before the Second World War Britain had been known as the 'World's Banker', the country that loaned more money to other nations than any other. By the end of the war in 1945 Britain owed huge amounts of money, mainly to the United States. To repay this debt politicians were desperate for the economy to recover from the war and begin to grow. Many of Britain's cities had been damaged by German bombing, and its railways, roads, ports and factories were all in need of modernization and improvement. But the country faced a new problem:

there were not enough workers to do all the work that was needed.

The year after the war ended, the British government estimated that the country needed an extra 1.3 million workers. One place they looked for those extra workers was in the camps that had been set up in Europe to house people who had lost their homes during the war. The people living there were known as 'Displaced Persons'. They were from Ukraine, Latvia, Estonia, Poland and other European countries. Thousands of them came to Britain and became known as European Volunteer Workers. They had no cultural connection to Britain and few of them spoke English but they were desperate to start new lives and happy to come to Britain. Thousands more people came from Ireland to help rebuild Britain and the British economy. But even though there was so much work to be done, and still not enough people to do it, the government did not want Black people from

> The year after the war ended, the British government estimated that the country needed an extra 1.3 million workers

the West Indies or Africa or people from India to come to Britain and help.

In 1945 there were probably fewer than 20,000 Black people in Britain. Although West Indians had been encouraged to come to Britain during the war, to serve in the armed forces and work in the factories, now that the war was over politicians of all political parties did not want Black people coming to Britain to find work and start new lives. The West Indians were not aware of the government's opposition. During the war they had been largely welcomed in Britain. When they went home to the West Indies after 1945 many found it impossible to get jobs and some decided to return to Britain. Britain needed workers, and as citizens of the British Empire they had the right to live and work in the UK. At school they had been taught that Britain was the 'mother country', the centre of the empire of which they were part. As people with skills who were willing and ready to work hard rebuilding the country, they expected they would be welcomed.

Windrush

On 21 June 1948 a ship called the *Empire Windrush* arrived at Tilbury Docks in London. It had travelled from Jamaica and on board were 492 Black people from across the islands of the West Indies. On the morning of 22 June the men and one woman on board disembarked and headed off to start their new lives in Britain. Many planned to stay in Britain for just a few years, to make some money and then go back to the West Indies. One of the newspapers, the *London Evening Standard*, celebrated their arrival in the imperial 'mother country'. The headline read 'Welcome home'. One of the men on board was Aldwyn Roberts, a famous singer from Trinidad whose stage name was Lord Kitchener. Before he left the *Empire Windrush* he sang his new song, 'London is the Place for Me' which was filmed by a camera crew from Pathé News.

The *Windrush* was just an average and unremarkable passenger ship, but it had an incredible backstory. It had been built in 1930, not in Britain but in Germany. Its original name was the MV *Monte Rosa* and between 1933

The Empire Windrush brought 492 West Indians to Britain in June 1948.

and 1939 it carried German families on cheap holiday cruises. Those holidays were arranged by an organization called Strength Through Joy, which was part of the Nazi Party. In 1939, the MV *Monte Rosa* became a troopship and was used to carry German soldiers into battle during the invasion of Norway. Later it transported Jewish people from Norway to Denmark. Most of those people were later deported to the extermination camp at Auschwitz-Birkenau where they were murdered by the Nazis. In 1944, the *Monte Rosa* was bombed by the RAF and in another incident had mines attached to its hull by members of the Norwegian Resistance, who were fighting the Germans. The ship survived both attacks but in 1945 it was captured by British forces and became the property of Britain. It was then that it was renamed the *Empire Windrush*. It is strange to think that the ship that has became the symbol of modern, multiracial Britain was once operated by a Nazi organization in a state that believed in racial purity and white racial supremacy.

> The ship that has became the symbol of modern, multiracial Britain was once operated by a Nazi organization

Although the British newspapers welcomed the people on the *Windrush*, in secret the British government was frustrated that they had come to Britain. Even before the *Windrush* had left Jamaica the government had tried to prevent the people on board from reaching Britain. The British Prime Minister Clement Attlee had made enquiries to see if the ship could instead be sent to East Africa, and the West Indian migrants could be offered work on a farming project that had been established in Tanganyika to grow peanuts for export to Britain. Three weeks before the *Windrush* arrived, the Minister of Labour, George Isaacs, reminded his colleagues in government that those on board the *Windrush* had not been officially invited to Britain and warned that 'the arrival of these substantial numbers of men under no organized arrangement is bound to result in considerable difficulty and disappointment'. A civil servant at the Home Office wrote that 'sooner or later action must be taken to keep out the undesirable elements of our colonial population'. On the day the

'Sooner or later action must be taken to keep out the undesirable elements of our colonial population'

Empire Windrush reached Tilbury Docks, eleven Labour MPs sent a letter to Attlee requesting that he put in place controls to limit Black immigration to Britain. In their letter they claimed that 'An influx of coloured people' coming to Britain would 'impair the harmony, strength and cohesion of our people and social life and cause discord and unhappiness among all concerned'.

After their arrival at Tilbury the people from the *Windrush* were housed in an old underground air-raid shelter in London. Within a month of their arrival all but twelve of the West Indians had found jobs and were hard at work in industries across the country. Two hundred and ninety-six of them had stayed in London; the others had moved to Liverpool, Manchester, Birmingham, Bristol, Plymouth, Leeds, Bolton, Colchester, and Birkenhead. One of the reasons they found work so quickly is that the people on the *Windrush* had exactly the skills Britain desperately needed in 1948. The passenger list of the *Windrush* tells us the names of the people on board but it also lists their skills. On the ship were eighty-five mechanics, fifty-four

West Indian migrants temporarily housed in an air-raid shelter beneath Clapham Common in south London.

carpenters, thirty-nine clerks, thirty-four tailors, twenty-three welders, twenty engineers, eighteen cabinet makers, eighteen students, fifteen machinists, fourteen fitters, thirteen electricians, twelve civil servants and ten shoemakers, as well as three boxers, two piano repairers, two hairdressers, a potter and a hatter.

During the summer of 1948, while the *Empire Windrush* had been crossing the Atlantic Ocean, a new law had been passing through Parliament. The British Nationality Act ensured that the people of the British Empire had the right to enter and live in Britain. It also ensured that people in Britain were free to emigrate and find new homes in the empire. But the MPs who passed the new law imagined that the people coming to Britain would be white people from Canada, South Africa, Australia and New Zealand – parts of the empire that were sometimes called the 'white dominions' or the 'old commonwealth'. However, the British Nationality Act gave the same rights to the people of what was called the 'new commonwealth', which included Africa and the West Indies, as well as Asia. The politicians believed that very few Black and brown people from those parts of the British Empire would come to Britain. They were wrong. By 1958, ten years after the *Windrush* had landed at Tilbury Docks, there were about 125,000 West Indian people living and working in Britain. During the same period 350,000 Irish people and around

> Politicians believed that very few Black and brown people from those parts of the British Empire would come to Britain. They were wrong

90,000 European Voluntary Workers had migrated to Britain.

Despite the opposition of the government throughout the 1950s, British companies were very happy to employ Black migrants. Some companies went out to the West Indies to set up offices through which they recruited people to come and work for them. In 1956 London Transport, the company that ran the buses and the tube trains in London, began to recruit new members of staff on the island of Barbados. London Transport even loaned money to the men and women it recruited to help pay for the costs of travelling to Britain. The National Health Service recruited nurses in the West Indies and by 1965 there were somewhere between 3,000 and 5,000 nurses from Jamaica alone hard at work in Britain's hospitals. Hotels and restaurants also recruited Black people from the West Indies to come to Britain and work for them.

> Some companies went out to the West Indies to set up offices through which they recruited people to come and work for them

Although almost half of the West Indian men and one in five of the women who came to Britain in the ten years after the *Windrush* had arrived were trained to do skilled jobs, many of them were disappointed to discover that the only work they were able to get in Britain was doing unskilled jobs. Their talents and their training, which Britain had found useful during the war years, were often disregarded. Many also faced terrible discrimination at work. At times white people refused to work alongside their new Black colleagues and whole companies decided not to hire Black workers. This was known as the 'colour bar'. In Bristol the local bus company refused to give jobs to Black and Asian people. In response, a group of West Indians in Bristol organized a boycott of the bus service in 1963. Black and Asian people, along with white people who supported them, refused to use the buses. This cut the company's profits and made the company's colour bar a big story that was reported in the newspapers and on television. In the end the boycott worked, and the bus company agreed to employ drivers and bus conductors from the West Indies, Pakistan and India.

The Black people who had come to Britain in the 1950s and 1960s were also deeply disappointed and hurt when they discovered how difficult it was to find somewhere to live. Many landlords would not rent flats or rooms to Black people, and so thousands of Black migrants had no choice but to look for rooms in the poorest parts of Britain's cities. Some were forced to rent rooms from corrupt landlords who charged very high rents for damp and dirty rooms. The result of this is that many Black people paid far more than white people for similar accommodation. As the prices were so high people had to share rooms and live in overcrowded accommodation.

Many landlords would not rent flats or rooms to Black people

In almost every aspect of their lives the Black migrants faced racism and discrimination. Sam King, one of the men who had come to Britain on the *Windrush*, felt that a 'third of people in Britain still had imperialist ideas', such as that 'People from the colonies should be planting bananas and chocolate and whatever it is'. Another third, he believed, were mildly hostile to Black migration, and the final third were what he called 'nice, ordinary people' who did not hold racist views. Sam King had first come to Britain during the Second World War and had served in the RAF. He was appalled by the racism he suffered, but despite it he became the first Black mayor of the London borough of Southwark in 1983.

Sam King MBE in 2004.

Throughout the 1950s British politicians remained opposed to the migration of Black people to Britain. The Marquess of Salisbury, who was a member of Winston's Churchill's government, said that the arrival of large numbers of Black people posed a threat to 'the racial character of the English people'. In 1954 Churchill himself warned one of his colleagues that if West Indian migration continued, 'we would have a magpie society: that would never do.' During this period governments run by both the Conservative and the Labour party carried out investigations into the Black community and had the police and others write reports about them.

> **Throughout the 1950s British politicians remained opposed to the migration of Black people to Britain**

While migrants from Europe were described in Parliament as 'first-class people who if let into this country would be of great benefit to our stock' and as people full of 'the spirit and stuff of which we can make Britons', Black men and women from the West Indies were described in government reports as 'unreliable and lazy' and part of an 'immigration problem'.

Race Relations

In 1958 violence broke out in the city of Nottingham and later in the Notting Hill area of London. In both cases the disturbances were called riots, but in reality they were attacks against Black people and their homes carried out by gangs of young white men. In Nottingham a group of white men attacked a Black man who had been seen talking with a white woman in a bar. For several hours West Indians in Nottingham were attacked by around a thousand white men; eight people were hospitalized. One week later in Notting Hill 400 mainly young, white men attacked local Black people and their homes. Many of the white men involved in the Notting Hill riots came from other parts of London. The violence took place over several nights, and over 140 people were arrested by the police. The Black people of Notting Hill, some of whom had fought in the war, came together and fought to defend their community. In doing so, they were assisted by a few of their white neighbours. Much of the press and a number of politicians blamed Black people for the disturbances.

Notting Hill, 3 September 1958. Police search a Black man on Talbot Road.

Long before the riots of 1958, politicians in Britain had wanted to change the law to make it more difficult for Black people to come and settle in Britain. After the violence, they believed that public opinion had changed and was now more hostile towards Black migration. Politicians of all parties felt able to openly call for controls to be introduced to reduce the number of Black people allowed to come to Britain, even though Black people from the West Indies and Africa and people from Asia were all citizens of the British Commonwealth.

> Politicians of all parties felt able to openly call for controls to be introduced to reduce the number of Black people allowed to come to Britain

In 1962 the government of Prime Minister Harold Macmillan passed a new immigration law. Under the Commonwealth Immigrants Act only people who had been issued with employment vouchers were able to enter the UK from the Commonwealth. The 1962 Act was careful to restrict the number of vouchers available for the sorts of jobs Black people typically did. This meant that while the new law had the effect of limiting the number of Black people able to come and work in Britain, it did not significantly affect the migration of white people from places like Australia and Canada. The law was deliberately designed to limit Black migration but do so in a way that was subtle and that made no mention of race. It turned people who under the 1948 British Nationality Act had been British subjects into immigrants. Seven years later William Deedes, who had been a minister in the Macmillan government that had passed the new law, admitted that the 1962 Act's 'real purpose was to restrict the influx of coloured immigrants. We were reluctant to say as much openly.'

The leader of the Labour Party, Hugh Gaitskell, condemned the Commonwealth Immigrants Act as, 'cruel and brutal anti-colour legislation'. But when Labour came to power in 1964 they did not abolish the act. Instead the new Labour government actually reduced the numbers of employment vouchers available to unskilled migrants, making it even harder for non-white people to come to Britain or for those already in the country to bring over their children or partners. Further immigration acts from 1968 to 1971 removed the last remnants of the rights of entry and residence that had been awarded to Commonwealth citizens by the 1948 British Nationality Act.

At the same time that British governments were trying to reduce the number of people from the Commonwealth coming to Britain, they were also trying to reduce the levels of discrimination against the Black migrants within British society. In 1965 and in 1968 the Labour government introduced two new Race Relations acts. The 1965 Race Relations Act set up the Race Relations Board which was given the task of investigating

> **They were also trying to reduce the levels of discrimination against the Black migrants within British society**

cases of racial discrimination. The law also made it illegal to discriminate against people on the grounds of their race in hotels, pubs, restaurants, theatres and nightclubs. Another part of the act made it illegal to incite racial hatred. However, the 1965 act did not outlaw discrimination in housing and employment – two of the most important areas of life. This meant that even after the act had become law, landlords were still able to publish advertisements for rooms to rent that said 'No Blacks'. The 1968 Race Relations Act established the Community Relations Commission and did make it illegal to discriminate in housing, employment and in access to loans from banks. But discrimination continued in more subtle ways.

'Rivers of Blood'

It was in opposition to the Labour government's plan to introduce the 1968 Race Relations Act that the Conservative MP Enoch Powell gave one of the most infamous speeches in British political history. In April 1968, two weeks after Martin Luther King had been assassinated in the United States, Powell delivered his so-called 'Rivers of Blood' speech. In it he described Black British children as 'wide-grinning piccaninnies' and said that Black people and Asian people, even if they were born in Britain, could never really be British. As racial outsiders Powell believed Black people should not be protected from racial discrimination with anti-racism laws but marginalized and ideally deported – Powell called it 're-emigration'. Refusing to see Black children who had been born in Britain as Britons, Powell called them the 'immigrant-descended population'. Later in

A photo taken eleven days after Enoch Powell's infamous 'Rivers of Blood' speech.

1968, in another speech, Powell said, 'The West Indian or Indian does not, by being born in England, become an Englishman. In law he becomes a United Kingdom citizen by birth; in fact he is a West Indian or an Asian still.'

Within a day of delivering his 'Rivers of Blood' speech Powell was sacked by his party, but huge numbers of people in Britain supported him. A poll taken in April 1968 reported that 74 per cent of those questioned agreed with

Powell was sacked by his party, but huge numbers of people in Britain supported him him. He received many of letters of support. The newspapers reported an increase in violence against non-white people in the weeks after the speech and many Black British people who lived through 1968 remember there being a dramatic change in how they were treated.

'Institutional racism'

By the middle of the 1970s four out of every ten Black people living in Britain had been born in the country. This younger generation constantly encountered racism in everyday life. At school Black Britons were discriminated against by a system that was quick to dismiss their intelligence and to place them in lower classes. Teachers often had low expectations of what Black people could achieve academically. After leaving school many were unable to find jobs because many employers remained prejudiced against Black people. Throughout the 1970s young Black British people also suffered at the hands of the police. Many reports were published that revealed how police forces across Britain harassed the Black community. Black youth clubs and nightclubs were constantly raided and Black political organizations were the subject of investigations and surveillance. Research carried out by sociologists into the internal culture found within the police revealed widespread racism. Black people were treated with suspicion and hostility, and racial slurs were used to describe them. When Black people were the victims of attacks by racists, the police often did little to help them or would reject the idea that racial prejudice had been the motivation of the attackers. When Black people were charged by the police, judges and juries in court almost always believed the police and their account of events.

In 1981 thirteen young people, all of them Black, died when a house in the New Cross area of London was consumed by fire. They had been attending a birthday party. The police ruled out the possibility that the fire had been started deliberately and, when pushed by the families, they dismissed suggestions that if the fire had been an arson attack there might have been racial motives behind it. There was silence from the political class and a strong sense among Black Londoners that the authorities were not interested in the deaths of young Black people. When, in March 1981, around 20,000 Black people marched from Deptford in South London to the centre of the city demanding a thorough investigation, sections of the press reported the predominantly peaceful march as a day of riots.

Grieving protestors march from New Cross to the House of Commons in 1981, after thirteen young Black people were killed in a fire at Deptford in south London.

The next month the Metropolitan Police began an operation against violent street crime in the Brixton area of London – home to a large Black community. By 1981 that community had run out of patience after years of harassment and vilification. That police operation, which was launched in April 1981, made use of the hated 'sus' law. The official term for this law was Section 4 of the Vagrancy Act of 1824, a law that had been passed over 150 years earlier under the reign of George IV. It was a law that William Wilberforce had been a critic of at the time. As used by the Metropolitan Police, the sus law allowed officers to stop and search anyone merely on the suspicion that they intended to commit a crime. The operation in Brixton was undertaken by the Special Patrol Group, a unit of the Metropolitan Police that had a terrible reputation among London's Black community, and the police named their operation 'Swamp 81', possibly after a speech Margaret Thatcher had given

> The sus law allowed officers to stop and search anyone merely on the suspicion that they intended to commit a crime

two years earlier in which she had said that 'some people have felt swamped by immigrants'.

Over two days, 120 police officers stopped and searched 943 people, arresting 118 on various charges. Tensions between the police and the Black community were already high and Swamp 81 led to a complete breakdown of trust and an explosion of anger and frustration. Years of resentment against the Special Patrol Group, and a legal system that routinely believed racist police officers and disbelieved members of the black community, had finally boiled over. The riots of 1981 spread beyond London to other cities and the areas of them in which young Black people, the children of the original *Windrush* generation, were marginalized and persecuted by the police. Riots broke out in Handsworth in Birmingham, Moss Side in Manchester, and Toxteth in Liverpool. In Liverpool young Black people rioted against a police force that for decades had been hostile towards them. The Liverpool Police 'task force' had a particularly bad reputation among Black Liverpudlians and had also

Toxteth in 1981.

made use of the sus law. Liverpool Chief Constable Kenneth Oxford believed that the cause of the riots was not police harassment or the effects of high unemployment but 'the problem of half-castes in Liverpool'. In Bristol, not far from the flickering flames of the riots in the St Paul's district of the city, a statue of Edward Colston, a slave trader and member of the Royal African Company in the seventeenth century, looked on.

The riots of the 1980s have been called 'uprisings' and they were a response to years of persecution and prejudice. They were destructive and in some ways damaging but they were understandable. A generation who had been targeted and harassed by the police their entire lives had simply had enough.

> A generation who had been targeted and harassed by the police their entire lives had simply had enough

In the years that followed, survey after survey plotted the decline in racist attitudes in Britain as a younger generation emerged who had not experienced the racism of the post-war period nor been brought up to view the world through the memory of the empire. Yet Black people still suffered higher rates of unemployment, achieved lower results at school, and were largely locked out of professional jobs in law, medicine, politics and the media. Hostility from the police also remained. In 1993, during this period in which life got better in many ways for Black Britons, a Black teenager called Stephen Lawrence was murdered by a gang of five white men.

Although his murderers were quickly identified and arrested, the police failed to prosecute them and the Lawrence family had to launch a private prosecution. The failures of the police to properly investigate the murder of Stephen Lawrence and prosecute his killers led to a public inquiry. The report that came from that inquiry was known as the Macpherson Report. What it showed was that the inaction of the police in seeking to prosecute the murderers of Stephen Lawrence was a symptom of a culture of 'institutional racism' within the Metropolitan Police.

The inaction of the police in seeking to prosecute the murderers of Stephen Lawrence was a symptom of a culture of 'institutional racism'

The history of Black people in Britain after 1945 was not just about immigration control, racism and the police. Although British racism, the ideas created by the slave owners of the eighteenth century and the empire builders of the nineteenth century, continued to impact on the lives of Black people, the story of Black British people was also one of culture, art, sport, integration and advancement. In the decades after 1980 the Black community grew in size and became increasingly African. At the turn of the century West Indians still made up the majority of the UK's Black population. But, as the 2011 census revealed, between 2001 and 2011 the British African population doubled, through both migration and natural increase. For the first time, probably, since the age of the Atlantic slave trade, the majority of Black Britons or their parents had come to this country directly from Africa, rather than from somewhere in the Americas. These newer migrants came mainly from West Africa; many were Nigerians or Ghanaians. Some came initially to study but ended up staying. Others migrated to join family and set up home, or to take up employment in a Britain that was still hungry for skilled workers. Like the West Indian nurses who came in the 1950s and 1960s, many of these migrants came to work in the National Health Service. Some of those who arrived from Somalia, Zimbabwe and Sudan came as refugees.

Between 2001 and 2011 the British African population doubled

While the British African population expanded, the longer established West Indian population integrated more successfully than perhaps any other immigrant group of modern times. West Indians have drawn millions of white British people, and people of other heritage, into their family networks through inter-marriage and friendships. At the same time they and the African migrants have also drawn the whole nation towards their cultures and music. Through sports, music, cinema, fashion and television, Black Britons became the standard-bearers of a new cultural and national identity. The Notting Hill Carnival, invented by the Trinidadian journalist Claudia Jones, initially in response to the Notting Hill riots of 1958, has become the biggest street festival in Europe and an established part of the calendar for Londoners. Many of the nations' sporting teams have become increasingly diverse and in doing so look increasingly like the home nations they represent.

Another critical feature of Black British life in the last years of the twentieth century was a determination within the

> Another critical feature of Black British life in the last years of the Twentieth century was a determination within the community to reclaim their lost history

community to reclaim their lost history. Because of the attitudes of men like Enoch Powell, who could not bring himself to see Black Britons as British, history was needed to demonstrate that Black British children, born of immigrant parents, were part of a longer story that stretched back to the Afro-Romans whose remains are only now being properly identified. In the 1980s the concept of Black History Month was brought to Britain – an idea that had been pioneered in the United States back in the 1920s, as 'Negro History Week'. Black History became critical to a whole community, while at the same time being highly personal to those who discovered it. At first Black History Month was dominated by African-American history but year by year has become more properly focused on the Black British past.

CONCLUSION

The 492 people from the West Indies who arrived on the *Empire Windrush* in 1948 were unaware that the cities in which they built their new lives – London, Liverpool, Bristol – had been the home to previous generations of Black Britons. In 1948 the historical research that was to later uncover the lives of the forgotten Black Tudors, Georgians and Victorians was yet to be done. Without knowing it, the *Windrush* pioneers walked in the footsteps of John Blanke, Olaudah Equiano, Mary Prince, Ignatius Sancho, Julius Soubise, Phillis Wheatley, Ottobah Cugoano, Francis Barber, Jonathan Strong, James Somerset, Dido Elizabeth Belle, Mary Seacole, Sarah Forbes Bonetta and Walter Tull. Had that history been available, it would have been understood that their arrival was just another chapter in a longer history. During the difficult years after 1948, when they were subjected to so much discrimination and suffered so much disadvantage, that same knowledge might have helped them rebuff the arguments put forward by those like Enoch Powell who rejected the idea that Black people could ever truly be British.

Six decades later, at the opening ceremony of the 2012 London Olympic Games, Britain celebrated the nation's culture and history. The opening ceremony revelled in Britain's diversity, music and youth culture, but it also sought to retell the national story. The Industrial Revolution, the First World War, the campaigns of the Suffragettes, the Jarrow March of 1936 and the creation of the NHS in 1948 were all celebrated in the opening ceremony. Alongside those landmarks in British history was the *Windrush*, in the form of a mock-up miniature of the ship. This replica was made of a metal frame around which had been stretched fabric printed with the covers of hundreds of post-war British newspapers. This

A mock-up of the Empire Windrush *at the Opening Ceremony of the 2012 Olympics.*

metal-framed, cloth-covered *Windrush* had smoke billowing from its two funnels and it was accompanied on a procession around the Olympic stadium by a group of twenty-first-century Black Londoners. Dressed in baggy 1940s-style suits and trilby hats, they carried leather suitcases of the sort their ancestors had arrived with sixty years earlier, and which can be seen stacked up on porter's trolleys and on the platforms of English railway stations in many of the black-and-white photographs from that time.

In 1948, when the *Windrush* arrived, there had been, at most, a few thousand Black Londoners. Today Britain's Black population stands at around 2 million, a little more than 3 per cent of the national total. Over a million Black people have made their homes in London, becoming part of the most diverse city on earth. The *Windrush*, the ship that has become the symbol of post-war migration and multicultural Britain, has become a part of the British national story, part of the vocabulary of the nation. There is a Windrush Square in Brixton, a heritage plaque in Tilbury marks the spot where the ship docked and the West Indian migrants came ashore, and a musical based on the lives and ambitions of the *Windrush* migrants enjoyed a successful run in London's West End. Since 2018, the seventieth anniversary of the arrival of the *Windrush*, 22 June has been designated Windrush Day. Yet despite all this, six years after the *Windrush* was celebrated in the opening ceremony at the London Olympic Games, the Guardian newspaper uncovered what became known as the Windrush Scandal.

Under what was called the 'hostile environment', thousands of British people of West Indian heritage, most of whom had come to Britain, often as children, in the 1960s and 1970s, had been stripped of their British citizenship. Many had lost their jobs, and when unable to pay their rent or mortgage, some had lost their homes. Others had been denied medical treatment in the same National Health Service hospitals that their parents' generation had worked in. Some had even been placed in detention centres or even deported back to countries they had not set foot in since they were children and in which they had no friends or family. Those deported were not allowed to return to the UK.

> Thousands of British people of West Indian heritage, most of whom had come to Britain, often as children, in the 1960s and 1970s, had been stripped of their British citizenship

The victims of the Windrush Scandal were people who had been given the automatic right to remain in the UK on arrival in the 1960s and early 1970s, but to whom no documents were ever issued to prove their status as British citizens. After living in Britain for decades and having worked and paid their taxes throughout their lives, they were suddenly stripped of their British citizenship. The Home Office had been warned years earlier that immigration policy was affecting older people from the West Indies but those warnings were ignored. When the scandal was revealed, the Black MP David Lammy, himself the son of Black migrants from Guyana, described the Windrush Scandal as a 'national day of shame'.

Two years later, in 2020, following the murder of George Floyd, an African-American man, a series of Black Lives Matter protests spread across the world. Thousands of people in Britain, most of them young, many of them still at school, organized protests and marched against racism. In Bristol young protesters who were aware of that city's historical role in the Atlantic Slave Trade pulled down a statue of Edward Colston, a seventeenth-century slave trader. Colston had been Deputy Governor of the Royal African Company. In that role Colston had been partially responsible for the enslavement and deaths of tens of thousands of Africans, yet his statue had stood in the centre of Bristol for 125 years. After it was toppled from its pedestal by protestors, the statue was dragged through the streets of Bristol and dumped into Bristol Harbour.

The fall of Colston marked the symbolic arrival of a new generation of young Black Britons who, along with white allies, are committed to fighting against the racism that still exists throughout much of British society. One of the ways in which they have sought to combat racism is to call for the teaching of Black British history in schools and universities.

GLOSSARY

Aballava a Roman fort in Cumbria where a whole community of people lived

Abolitionists a group of people who campaigned to end slavery

American Patriots Americans who were rebelling against British rule, during the late 1700s (around the time of the American War of Independence)

Atlantic Slave Trade the period between 1640-1807 where around three and a half million people from Africa were enslaved and taken to America and the West Indies by the British

Barbados Slave Code the laws setting out the system in which enslaved people were forced to live on the island of Barbados

Bill (government) the formal proposal for a new law

Billet a place where soldiers temporarily live

Black Pioneers a regiment of slaves formerly owned by Americans who fought for the British during the American War of Independence

The Black Poor a term used to describe slaves formerly owned by Americans, who fought for the British during the American War of Independence and subsequently lived in Britain. But as most had no money or people who were willing to help them, they were left homeless and lived in terrible conditions

Blackface a form of racism where white people wear dark makeup to mimic and stereotype Black people

Blockade the act of blocking off a certain location so that food and other goods cannot enter, to try to cause a huge strain to that place

Boycott to give up or avoid a person or an organisation for social or political reasons

British Empire the group of countries (colonies) that the British ruled

The British Nationality Act a law that said people who lived in countries that the British had colonized (i.e. countries that were part of the British Empire) had the right to enter and live in Britain. It also ensured that people in Britain were free to emigrate and find new homes in other countries within the empire.

Census an official government survey that gathers the details and personal information of every person in a population

Colonies a group of people of one nationality or race who settle in a new place but keep cultural ties to their homeland

Colonize to establish control over another country

Conscription a system that a government can put in place to force people to join the army

The colour bar a system that denies Black people the same rights as white people

Dysentery an internal infection that can cause severe diarrhoea

Emancipation the process of being set free, specifically in terms of enslaved people

Ethiopian Regiment a regiment of slaves formerly owned by Americans who fought for the British during the American War of Independence

European Volunteer Workers people from European countries who came to Britain to find work after the end of WWII

Freetown what is now the capital city of Sierra Leone, where 'recaptive' people settled in 1792

Garrison a group of soldiers who are stationed in a town to defend it

GI a US soldier in Britain during WWII

Gradualism the idea that slavery had to be ended gradually, over many years, rather than stopped immediately

Hanoverian a royal house that ruled Britain and Ireland between 1714 and 1901

Hue and Cry a newspaper advertisement that offered rewards for the recapture of slaves who had escaped their masters

Immigrant a person who comes to live permanently in a country different to the one in which they were born

Indentured servants poor people and prisoners who were signed up to work without pay for a period of seven to nine years. They were often very badly treated, but once their time was up they were free again.

Labour corps an organisation that provides military-related labour

Middle Passage the horrific voyage that enslaved Africans were forced to take across the Atlantic Ocean

Migrant a person who moves from one country to the other, usually in order to find work or better living conditions

Minstrels white performers who painted their faces black to copy the music and dancing of enslaved Americans

Missionary a person who travels to a foreign country to promote a certain religion, often Christianity

Moors a term used in the Middle Ages meaning 'people from North Africa'

'New racism' racism that appeared in the second half of the nineteenth century, that used science to try to justify racism

Ottoman Empire a state that controlled a large part of Northern Africa, Western Asia and South eastern Europe between the 14th and early 20th centuries

Palavers a meeting between two groups of people

Plantation a large estate or piece of land used for farming crops on a large scale, such as cotton, tea or sugar cane

Proclamation a public announcement, usually of great importance

Protectorate a country that is protected by another, usually stronger, country

Province of Freedom a settlement in Sierra Leone

Quaker a branch of Christianity that is specifically devoted to peaceful principles

Race Relations Act a set of British laws that made certain forms of racism illegal

Regiment a military unit

Royal African Company an English company that traded enslaved people

Recaptives enslaved people who were 'twice captured'. They were initially captured in Africa to be transported across the Atlantic, but were subsequently captured by the Royal Navy and set free

Sarcophagus a stone coffin, often decorated with art or inscriptions

Segregation a system that forces people from different races to be separate from one another

Social Darwinism a theory used to justify political racism, based on Darwin's theory of evolution. It stated that Black people are inferior to white people

Sons of Africa a group of Black British abolitionists, who had either formerly been slaves or who were the children of enslaved parents

Sugar cane a plant from which sugar is extracted

The sus law a British law that allows the Metropolitan Police to stop and search anyone merely on the suspicion that they intended to commit a crime

Tsarina empress of Russia

West Indies a term coined by colonising European powers to refer to the 7000 islands of the Caribbean